BURT FRANKLIN: RESEARCH & SOURCE WORKS SERIES
Selected Studies in History, Economics, and Social Science
n.s. 19c (Modern European Studies)

PURITANISM

IN ENGLAND

PURITANISM
IN ENGLAND

BY

H. HENSLEY HENSON, D.D.

CANON AND SUB-DEAN OF WESTMINSTER
SOMETIME FELLOW OF ALL SOULS COLLEGE, OXFORD

BURT FRANKLIN
NEW YORK

Published by LENOX HILL Pub. & Dist. Co. (Burt Franklin)
235 East 44th St., New York, N.Y. 10017
Reprinted: 1972
Printed in the U.S.A.

Burt Franklin: Research and Source Works Series
Selected Studies in History, Economics, and Social Science
  n.s. 19c (Modern European Studies)

Reprinted from the original edition in the Princeton University
  Library.

Library of Congress Cataloging in Publication Data

Henson, Herbert Hensley, Bp. of Durham, 1863-1947.
  Puritanism in England.

  Reprint of the 1912 ed.
  1. Puritans—England. I. Title.
BX9334.H37 1972   285'.9'0942   70-185944
ISBN 0-8337-4177-2

PREFACE

THE six lectures here published were delivered in Westminster Abbey on Friday afternoons during Lent this year. They are published without alteration. The circumstances of haste and pressure in which they were composed are sufficiently disclosed by their slightness and penury of reference. But the opinions and judgments they express have not been arrived at quickly, or without labour.

I have added three Sermons which bear more or less directly on the main theme, and will serve to supply some lacunæ in the Lectures. They were delivered respectively in Westminster

Abbey, in the Crypt of Canterbury Cathedral, and in the University Church, Cambridge.

In choosing 'Puritanism' for the subject of my Lenten Lectures I was influenced by the circumstance that Nonconformists generally were engaged in commemorating the 250th anniversary of the Ejectment of their religious ancestors. I trust that nothing has been said which can fairly be regarded as lacking in sympathy or appreciation for the Victims of what I must needs consider the meanest persecution which Christian History records. Nevertheless, I cannot think that the tradition of their sufferings ought to be allowed to raise the temperature of modern discussions, or to suggest a polemic for modern controversialists.

H. HENSLEY HENSON.

WESTMINSTER ABBEY,

CONTENTS

CONTENTS

ELIZABETHAN PURITANISM

I

ELIZABETHAN PURITANISM

TWO hundred and fifty years have passed since the Nonconformist clergy, about two thousand in number if we accept the contemporary estimates, were ejected from their benefices by the Act of Uniformity (1662).

It is, perhaps, no more than we ought to expect that so important and tragic an event—important in its consequences, tragic in its incidents—should be made the subject of commemoration by those who regard themselves as the religious representatives of the ejected Puritans. Yet we cannot avoid a certain anxiety lest the commemoration should take a polemical aspect, and thus have the unfortunate effect of rekindling the failing fires of religious strife, and giving new life to old and now moribund prejudices. For it is unhappily the case that the exasperating memories of 1662 can hardly be revived in 1912 without connecting themselves unwholesomely with the actual process of politics. With Disestablishment actually in debate, it is not hard to see that the renewed study of the crisis in which the existing Establishment of the Church of England was effected, with much persecuting violence, may lend itself more easily and obviously to the service of political invective than to that of any worthier interest. This would be the more unfortunate since a candid and unprejudiced review of this chapter of our religious history might well contribute much to the discipline and guidance of the modern Church, as well established as non-established. It occurred to me, therefore, that it might be profitable, and could hardly be unfitting, if we were to devote these Lenten lectures to the attempt to consider English Puritanism without controversial *arrière-pensée*, or denominational prejudice. In WESTMINSTER, if anywhere, such an attempt ought to be legitimate and hopeful, for there the most stirring episodes of the brief Puritan domination were witnessed, and within the walls of the Abbey was framed the most widely accepted of Puritan Confessions.

'Puritan,' like 'Christian,' 'Huguenot,' and 'Quaker,' is a nickname, originally devised as a term of abuse and expressing general contempt, which in the course of time has been made honourable by the associations of virtue and heroism which have gathered about it, and has thus come to be a source of legitimate pride to those who have the right to bear it. The ecclesiastical writers of the seventeenth century, HEYLYN and FULLER, agree in referring its origin to the early years of ELIZABETH, when the system of the Reformed Church was being set up in circumstances of extraordinary difficulty and confusion. In the preface to the Puritan manifesto called the 'Admonition to the Parliament,' published by CART-WRIGHT in 1572, complaint is made that the Bishops 'link in together, and slanderously charge poor men with grievous faults, calling them Puritans, worse than the Donatists.' When GRINDAL, Archbishop of York, in writing to the Puritan SAMPSON, spoke of 'the riot of Puritanism,' and referred with some scorn to those who held 'a Puritanism superstition,' he was roundly answered by his correspondent :—

'Yet do I not well understand what you do mean by those Puritans. Because you do use a dark phrase, noting them to hold a *pure* superstition. Till I be further instructed in this, I say, that if Puritans now be noted to be such as do revive the old rotten heresy of NOVATUS, from whom the old *Katharoi* did spring, I do not know any in England which do hold that desperate doctrine. . . . But unjustly to impose this name on brethren, with whose doctrine and life no man can justly find fault, is to rend the seamless coat of Christ, and to make a schism incurable in the church, and to lay a stumbling-block to the course of the Gospel.' [1]

HEYLYN gives the year 1565 as the actual date at which 'the Zwinglian or Calvinian faction began to be first known by the name of Puritans,' and he indicates its significance with characteristic bitterness :—

'Which name hath ever since been appropriate to them, because of their pretending to a greater purity in the service of God than was held forth

[1] v. Appendix xciv. to Strype's 'Life of Parker.'

unto them (as they gave it out) in the Common Prayer Book ; and to a greater opposition to the rites and usages of the Church of Rome than was agreeable to the constitution of the Church of England. But this purity was accompanied with such irreverence, this opposition drew along with it so much licentiousness, as gave great scandal and offence to all sober men.'[1]

FULLER, ascribing the first use of the name to the year 1564, gives a more discriminating account of its early application :—

'A name which, in this notion, first began in this year ; and the grief had not been great, if it had ended in the same. The philosopher banisheth the term (which is polysæmon) that is subject to several senses, out of the predicaments, as affording too much

[1] ' History of the Reformation,' ii. 421.

covert for cavill by the latitude thereof. On the same account could I wish that the word " Puritan " were banished common discourse, because so various in the acceptation thereof. We need not speak of the ancient Cathari or primitive Puritans sufficiently known by their heretical opinions. " *Puritan* " here was taken for the opposers of the hierarchy and church-service, as resenting of superstition. But profane mouths quickly improved this nickname, therewith on every occasion to abuse pious people : some of them so far from opposing the liturgy, that they endeavoured (according to the instructions thereof in the preparative to the Confession) " to accompany the minister with a *pure* heart," and laboured (as it is in the Absolution) " for a life *pure* and holy." We will, therefore, decline the word to prevent exceptions : which, if casually slipping from our pen, the reader knoweth that only nonconformists are thereby intended.' [1]

This character of ' Nonconformists' attached to all the Elizabethan Puritans, but it by no means meant in all cases the same thing. ' Nonconformity' might indicate no more than a conscientious dislike of specific details of the established system of the Church, as for instance kneeling at the Holy Communion, or the use of the Cross in Baptism ; or it might indicate a conscientious objection to Prelacy ; or it might even go to the length of a conscientious repudiation of the existing Church of England. Bishop COOPER in an often-quoted passage of his ' Admonition to the People of England,' published in 1589, has described the evolution of Puritanism. He wrote of course with the bias of an avowed opponent, but the substantial truth of his statements cannot be disputed :—

[1] v. ' Church History,' ii. 474.

'He that is the authour of all perillous alterations, and seeketh to worke mischief by them, will not attempt all at once, but will practise by little and little, and make every former feate that he worketh, to be a way and meane to draw on the residue. For he seeth all men will not be overcome with all temptations, nor will not be made instruments of all evill purposes, though happily by his colours and pretenses he be able to deceive them in some. The practise hereof, wee have seen in this Church of England, to the great trouble and danger thereof. At the beginning some learned and godly Preachers, for private respects in themselves made strange to weare the *Surplesse*, *Cap*, or *Tippet:* but yet so, that they declared themselves to thinke the thing indifferent, and not to judge evil of such as did use them. Shortly after rose up another, defending that they were not thinges indifferent, but distayned with Antichristian idolatrie, and therefore not to bee suffered in the Church. Not long after came forth an other sort, affirming that those matters touching Apparell, were but trifles, and not worthie contention in the Church, but that there were greater thinges farre of more weight and importance, and indeede touching faith and religion, and therefore meete to be altered in a Church rightly refourmed: As "the booke of Common Prayer, the administration of the Sacraments, the government of the Church, the election of Ministers," and a number of other like. Fourthly, now breake out another sort, earnestly affirming and teaching, that we have no Church, no Bishops, no Ministers, no Sacraments: and therefore that all they that love Jesus Christ, ought with all speede to separate them-selves from our congregation, because our assemblies are prophane, wicked, and Antichristian.'[1]

To this testimony of Bishop COOPER we may add that of RICHARD HOOKER in the Preface to his great work, where after speaking of the excessive authority which was being yielded to CALVIN throughout the Protestant Churches, he proceeds to describe the situation in England :—

'Amongst ourselves, there was in King EDWARD's days some question moved by reason of a few men's scrupulosity touching certain things. And beyond seas, of them which fled in the days of Queen MARY, some contenting themselves abroad with the use of their own service-book at home authorized before their departure out of the realm, others liking better the Common Prayer-book of the Church of Geneva translated, those smaller contentions before begun were by

[1] v. 'Admonition,' p. 131.   Reprint of 1847.

this means somewhat increased. Under the happy reign of her Majesty which now is (ELIZABETH), the greatest matter awhile contended for was the wearing of the cap and surplice, till there came Admonitions directed unto the high court of Parliament, by men who concealing their names thought it glory enough to discover their minds and affections, which now were universally bent even against all the orders and laws, wherein this church is found unconformable to the platform of Geneva. Concerning the Defender of which Admonitions (THOMAS CARTWRIGHT) all that I mean to say is but this : *there will come a time when three words uttered with charity and meekness shall receive a far more blessed reward than three thousand volumes written with disdainful sharpness of wit.* But the manner of men's writing must not alienate our hearts from the truth if it appear they have the truth ; as the followers of the same defender do think he hath ; and in that persuasion they follow him, no otherwise than himself doth CALVIN, BEZA, and others, with the like persuasion that they in this cause had the truth. We being as fully persuaded otherwise, it resteth that some kind of trial be used to find out which part is in error.' [1]

The evolution of Puritanism thus described is the salient feature of our ecclesiastical history during the reign of ELIZABETH, and has left its record in the two grand polemical duels of the time, that between CARTWRIGHT and WHITGIFT, and that between TRAVERS and HOOKER. The student of Puritanism must by no means omit a careful study of these memorable controversies.

Two factors must be distinguished in the earlier Puritanism, the one home-born,

[1] v. Preface to ' Eccl. Polity,' ii. 10.

the other of foreign extraction. The first goes back beyond the Reformation to the fourteenth century, when it grew from the preaching of JOHN WYCLIFFE. The last sprang from the intercourse with the foreign Reformers which began with CRANMER, and grew extremely close during the Marian persecution. Dr. GAIRDNER has reminded us in a recent work that Lollardism played a great part in the process of the English Reformation. It is hardly too much to say that the Reformation, so far as it was a popular movement, was a Lollard movement. From Lollardism, surviving as a tradition among the people, came the dynamic force of religious conviction, and the principle of ecclesiastical innovation. That principle—'the essential principle of Puritanism' as Dr. BRIGGS has called it not excessively—was the necessity of Scriptural authority for all ecclesiastical arrangements. As far back as the middle of the fifteenth century, Bishop PECOCK, anticipating RICHARD

HOOKER, had argued against the Lollards on this point. Archbishop CRANMER, writing in 1552 with reference to Puritan objections against the second Prayer-book (which though itself a monument of Puritan influence retained too much of the liturgical tradition to satisfy the more thorough-going Reformers), justly pointed to this mistaken exaltation of Scripture as the fount of ecclesiastical confusion : 'They say that kneeling is not commanded in Scripture : and what is not commanded in Scripture is unlawful. *There is the root of the errors of the sects!* If that be true, take away the whole Book of Service, and let us have no more trouble in setting forth an order in religion, or indeed in common policy. If kneeling be not expressly enjoined in Holy Scripture, neither is standing nor sitting. Let them lie down on the ground, and eat their meat like Turks or Tartars.' [1]

[1] v. Dixon, 'History of the Church of England,' iii. 476.

Not unconnected with their theory of the Scripture as the sole and sufficient authority for all ecclesiastical arrangements, was the practice of Psalm-singing, to which the Puritans gave an important place in public worship. Bishop JEWEL, writing to PETER MARTYR in 1560, observed on the popularity of Psalm-singing among the Londoners : ' You may see sometimes at Paul's Cross after the service six thousand persons, old and young, of both sexes, all singing together and praising God.' The practice received stimulus by the publication in 1562 of a complete metrical version under the now famous names of STERNHOLD and HOPKINS. The Puritans were, indeed, careful to draw a distinction between the traditional modes of praise and that which they approved. When WHITGIFT claimed agreement with his opponent on this point—' Singing I am sure you do not disallow, being used in all Reformed Churches, and an art allowed in Scriptures,

and used in praising God by David '—
CARTWRIGHT was at the pains to make
clear what precisely he understood by
allowable singing. He assumes that
WHITGIFT 'will not defend the piping and
organs, nor no other singing than is used
in the reformed Churches, which is, in
the singing of two psalms, one in the
beginning and another in the ending, in a
plain tune, easy both to be sung of those
which have no art in singing, and under-
standed of those which, because they
cannot read, cannot sing with the rest of
the church.'[1]   It was indeed fortunate for
the Puritans that they could find Scriptural
authority for psalm-singing, and even for
the use of musical instruments. They
never adopted the rigid attitude which
marked the Presbyterians of Scotland with
respect to the latter. The English people
have a natural fondness for music, and,
perhaps, no small natural aptitude for it.
Generally it may be observed that the

[1] v. Whitgift, Works, iii. 106, 7, P.S.

fervour which marked the congregational psalmody of the Reformed Churches indicates the sense of religious privation which the suppression of the medieval worship bred in the people. It is interesting to notice that the exemption enjoyed by music from the general proscription of the • arts enabled the Puritans of the next age to find in its cultivation some relief from the dour and melancholy habit to which their formal creed seemed to commit them.

The year 1572 is critical for Elizabethan Puritanism, for then the Puritan leaders adopted a policy which is difficult to defend in point of morality, and was pre-destined to defeat. At Wandsworth the Presbyterian system was actually estab-lished, and from that centre an organised effort to presbyterianise the Church of England from within was set on foot. 'This was the first-born of all presbyteries in England,' says FULLER, 'and *secundum usum Wandesworth* as much honoured by some as *secundum usum Sarum* by others.' We may conjecture that the Puritan leaders were misled by the Protestant fervour of the country into supposing that the time was favourable for a radical change in the ecclesiastical system. A profound impression had been made on the public mind by the violence of the Counter-Reformation on the Continent, a violence which culminated in the massacre of Huguenots in Paris on St. Bartholomew's Day, 1572. The rebellion of the northern earls had brought home to the people the danger in which the throne of ELIZABETH stood, and PIUS V.'s excommunication of the Queen had pointed out the direction from which that danger really arose. The year 1570 marks the formal separation of Roman Catholics from the National Church. It is significant that it should have been so quickly followed by a movement which indicated a separatist temper in the Puritans.

The inevitable consequence of the formal adoption of the Presbyterian Discipline was to drive a wedge into Puritanism. In their zeal the Puritan leaders ignored the national sentiment of their own nation, and drew upon themselves the suspicion and dislike which in that age never failed to come upon those who appeared to be unpatriotic. Incidentally, they wrecked an experiment which seemed to promise great religious results. The Prophesyings were the most conspicuous, and the most widely effective, of Puritan instruments.

It is worth while to consider briefly this short-lived but famous experiment. Archbishop GRINDAL, in his letter to the Queen (1576), when she called upon him to suppress the Prophesyings, pleaded earnestly for their continuance, as tending to increase the number of preachers and to improve their quality. These, from the Puritan point of view, were matters of primary importance. GRINDAL postulates that 'public and continual preaching of God's Word is the ordinary mean and instrument of the salvation of mankind,' ascribes the loyalty of London to 'the continual preaching of God's Word in that city,' and explains the recent rebellion of the North as the natural consequence of 'Papistry, and ignorance of God's Word through want of often preaching.' To the objection that many incompetent persons were admitted to preach, he replies by stating the precautions against incompetence which he was accustomed to adopt himself, and to press on his fellow-Bishops. 'We admit no man to the office that either professeth Papistry or Puritanism.' He points out that dislike of preaching went generally with disloyalty to the Reformation itself, and insists that 'Homilies set forth by public authority' could never really take the place of preaching. Nor, indeed—he reminds his impatient Sovereign—were they ever intended to do so, but only 'to supply necessity for want of preaching' in the numerous parishes, seven-eights of the whole number as he reckons, where 'no sufficient living for a learned preacher' was provided by the miserable endowment. Then he proceeds to attempt the removal of ELIZABETH'S prejudices by giving a detailed account of the Prophesyings, and setting out at length the arguments in their favour. Finally, taking his courage in both hands, he declares bluntly that his conscience will not allow him to carry out the Queen's wishes.

'For my own part, because I am very well assured, both by reasons and arguments taken out of the holy Scriptures, and by experience (the most certain seal of sure knowledge), that the said exercises, for the interpretation and exposition of the Scriptures, and for exhortation and comfort drawn out of the same, are both profitable to encrease knowledge among the Ministers, and tendeth to the edifying of the hearers, I am forced, with all humility, and yet plainly, to profess that I cannot with safe conscience, and without the offence of the majesty of God, give my assent to the suppressing of the said exercises; much less can I send out any injunction for the utter and universal subversion of the same.'

His closing appeal to the Queen is couched in a high and manly vein, and reflects the utmost credit on his character. It hardly needs saying that ELIZABETH was quite unable either to yield to its demand, or to pardon its audacity. GRINDAL was publicly disgraced, and the Prophesyings were suppressed. I have dwelt at such length on the Archbishop's letter because it illustrates the sober and religious Puritanism, which formed the soundest element in the Reformation, and had no worthier exponent than GRINDAL himself. For, though he disclaimed the name, GRINDAL was a representative Puritan, and his defence of the Prophesyings is undiluted Puritanism. Now, however, a change was taking place. As the inexorable attitude of the Queen's government destroyed all hope of any alteration in the established system, the more ardent Puritans turned against the system itself, and sought to realise their ecclesiastical ideal in independence of the constituted authorities, and in despite of them. The Prophesyings were a weapon ready to the hands of these bolder men, who did not scruple to utilise them for the establishment of the new presbyterian polity, which they had admired at Geneva, and now observed also in Scotland.

WHITGIFT and BANCROFT perceived the danger, and acted with ruthless but necessary severity. If the system of the National Church were to be preserved and made efficient, there could be no terms kept with a party which avowedly used its position within the system in order to destroy it and substitute another. With the Puritan statements before us, and the records of their actual proceedings, we cannot doubt that nothing less than a total revolution was intended. The late Bishop of Oxford, Dr. PAGET, whose decision was based on a thorough knowledge of the facts, and whose natural candour disinclined him to an undue severity, has stated the case with lucidity and care. He points out that CARTWRIGHT, TRAVERS, and their followers, holding benefices and acting under legal disguises, aspired to abolish episcopacy altogether, to destroy the Royal Supremacy and substitute a consistorial authority, to degrade from orders all the clergy who had received ordination from the Bishops under HENRY VIII. and MARY, and to make a clean sweep of everything in the Prayer-book which could not be shown to have explicit authority in Scripture.

'The scheme thus characterized was to be established and enforced by the authority of the Crown; it was to supersede the existing Church of England; it was to be the defined and authorized form of religion for the Queen's subjects; and neither the temper of the times, the nature and affinities of the scheme, nor the language of its champions promised much liberty of divergence from it.   There may have been much that was faulty in the arguments, the policy, the motives of those who opposed it, as well as much that was sincere and excellent in the enthusiasm of those who contended for it; the time was a time of tangled strife, and primary importance was often attached to subordinate matters; the points in controversy were multitudinous, and there was much misplacing of emphasis, and some stood out stiffly when they might have yielded wisely, and others claimed the shelter of authority for selfish interests and indefensible abuses. But through all the confusion and misunderstanding, the ultimate question at issue in the Puritan controversy of HOOKER's day was not whether the Prayer-book should be altered here and there, nor whether large allowance should be made for those who resented its requirements. It was a question which presupposed the conviction that the religious life of a nation must have a uniform expression ; it was the question whether the religious life of England should be expressed in the continuance of the historic Church of England, or in a system such as CALVIN had established at Geneva.' [1]

The Church of England in the closing years of ELIZABETH may be fairly described

[1] v. An Introduction to the Fifth Book of Hooker's 'Treatise of the Laws of Ecclesiastical Polity,' 53.

as a popular institution.   It had benefited
from the patriotic enthusiasm which filled
the nation after the long nightmare of
Spanish invasion had been for ever removed by the defeat of the Great Armada.
Time gave strength and dignity to the
religious settlement, which had at first
possessed little of either, bearing in the
eyes of a public, familiar with sudden
changes of religious policy, the ignoble
aspect of a merely provisional arrange-
ment.   From the death of HENRY VIII.
to the settlement of ELIZABETH was but
fourteen years, and in that short period
the system of Religion had been drasti-
cally changed no less than four times.   It
is no wonder that serious men, and such
the Puritans were beyond question, should
have regarded with slight respect a Church
which seemed to be the docile instrument
of the State, without principles or rights or
aspirations of its own.   Before ELIZABETH'S
reign had run its course, a new generation
of Anglicans had come on the scene, men

who had grown up in the use of the
Prayer-book, who had known no other
system than that which was powerfully
defended on its merits by WHITGIFT and
HOOKER, and which had become associated
in English minds both with stirring
national triumphs, and cherished domestic
experiences. An Anglican was no longer
necessarily a mere time-server, like that
typical Bishop KITCHEN of Llandaff, respecting whom the gibe passed on men's
lips that he could sing a new song to the
Lord four times in fourteen years, and yet
never sing out oᵢ tune. Moreover, the
gross practical abuses which disfigured it
were slowly being removed, as the system
of government gained strength, and a
new generation of better-trained clergy
came on the field. The destructive Puritanism which rebelled against the Bishops
and the Liturgy had been defeated, and
seems at the close of the reign to have
had but a small popular following; while
the more genuine Puritanism, which

accepted loyally the National Constitution in Church and State, had largely leavened the religious public. Already a distinction was being made in common speech between 'protestant' and 'puritan,' the former term being universally allotted to the Established Church, which in that age regarded itself, and was generally regarded by others, as the most conspicuous of Protestant Churches. In his elaborate work, published in 1910, on 'The Reconstruction of the English Church,' Dr. USHER has carefully investigated the assumed popularity of the Nonconformist Puritans, and the conclusions to which he has arrived are set forth in the chapter on 'The Attitude of the People towards the Church.' Taking the last year of ELIZABETH'S reign, he attempts to determine how many clergy were avowed Puritans, and what proportion of laymen may be fairly believed to have followed them. He has no difficulty in showing that the common estimates of both are greatly exaggerated. He tells us that 'the strength of the Puritan movement must have lain almost entirely in its clergy'; that 'it was a movement of the ministers and for the ministers, who heeded little the desires of their congregations'; that even on the contemporary and doubtless excessive Puritan estimate 'about two per cent. of the population will be enrolled as Puritans, leaving the rest to be divided between the Catholics and the Established Church'; that 'so far as there was any party, it was mainly composed in 1603 of about three hundred and fifty men, supported by the gentry and town corporations of their districts in the face of more or less apathetic congregations, having the adherence of perhaps fifty thousand able-bodied men pretty well distributed over the Eastern Counties, the Midlands, and the South.' He points out, indeed, that even so petty a number was more formidable than it appears, for 'seventy-five per cent. of the population were utterly indifferent to all forms of church government or details of ceremonies,' and probably at least five per cent. were avowed Catholics.

It must not, indeed, be supposed that acceptance of the established Church indicated in all cases a sincere approval of its system. Dr. USSHER goes so far as to say 'that there were probably not ten conscientious men in all England in 1603, who approved of the Church precisely as it stood,' but we must remember that conscientious men are but a minority at any time, and that ordinary Englishmen in the early seventeenth century still looked on the regulation of ecclesiastical arrangements as the proper work of the civil governor. Political questions were beginning to contest in English minds the supremacy which had so long been possessed by questions of religion, for the nation was becoming conscious of its powers, and becoming restive under the strong hand of the Queen, The change of dynasty would 'reveal the secrets of many hearts,' and remove the veil from many tendencies. WHITGIFT and BANCROFT succeeded in securing the provisional acceptance of the Established Church. Everything turned on the competence of the Established Church to make itself the instrument through which the new sensitiveness of the English conscience, and the new consciousness of political rights, would find expression. And this point would be inseparably connected with the question, which was presenting itself already to thoughtful minds, whether the new and unknown monarch would have the wisdom to read rightly the signs of the time, and the courage to follow the untrodden paths to which they pointed. There was a general expectation of ecclesiastical change. Men had held their hands from active agitation during the last years of the old Queen's life, partly out of deference to her venerable years, and partly from a conscious-

ness that her disappearance from the
scene of public life must needs precipitate
changes in the system which she embodied.
Puritans, moreover, cherished the belief
that a 'covenanted king' could not but be
favourable to them, and awaited with
strangely mistaken complacency the first
disclosures of his religious policy. The
wisest man in England, FRANCIS BACON,
thought that the time called for a serious
effort to satisfy the reasonable demands of
those who pointed to grave practical
defects in the Establishment. JAMES had
been more worthy of his description as
'the British Solomon' if he had taken to
heart the little tractate on Ecclesiastical
Reform which BACON placed in his hands
on his arrival in England. Time would
woefully disappoint the 'devout and fervent prayer' with which the author con-
cluded his recommendations, that as the
king had been made 'the corner stone
in joining his two kingdoms, so he
might be also as a corner stone to unite

and knit together the differences in the Church of God.' The reign of the first Stuart would witness the rise of a new kind of Puritanism, less unreasonable in its demands, and less capable of such handling as the traditional 'king-craft,' in which JAMES had been trained, could alone suggest.

PURITANISM BEFORE THE CIVIL WAR

II

PURITANISM BEFORE THE CIVIL WAR

THE religious Englishman of the later years of ELIZABETH sympathised with the Puritan attitude of thorough-going hostility to everything Roman, and perhaps cherished a theoretical belief in the ecclesiastical system of Geneva, but he distrusted and disliked the Puritan contempt of law and order. COLLIER relates that Lord BURLEIGH, perhaps the best representative of the religious English layman we can select, once invited the discontented dissenters from the Liturgy to 'draw up another, and contrive the offices in such a form as might give general satisfaction to their brethren. Upon this overture

'the first classis struck out their lines,
and drew mostly by the portrait of
Geneva. This draught was referred
to the consideration of a second
classis, who made no less than six
hundred exceptions to it. The third
classis quarrelled with the corrections
of the second, and declared for a new
model. The fourth refined no less
upon the third.'

In this situation the Puritans presented
an aspect sufficiently contemptible.

'Since they could not come to
any agreement in a form for Divine
Service, he had an handsome
opportunity of a release; for now they
could not decently importune him any
farther. To part smoothly with them,
he assured their agents, that when
they came to any unanimous resolve
upon the matter before them, they
might expect his friendship, and that

he should be ready to bring their scheme to a settlement.' [1]

The wily statesman had laid his hand on the weak point of militant Puritanism. It was incorrigibly anarchic, and that in an age which magnified before all things order and uniformity. Lord BURLEIGH was the spokesman of ordinary English citizens when he said that

> ' there could be no government where there was division ; that that State could never be in safety where there was a toleration of two religions ; that they that differ in the service of their God can never agree in the service of their country.' [2]

This state of mind might find one of two expressions. It would suggest a

[1] v. 'Ecclesiastical History,' ii. 586.
[2] v. 'The Compleat Statesman, a contemporary Life of Burleigh,' printed in Peck's *Desiderata Curiosa*, book i. p. 33. London, 1779.

policy of mere repression of all forms of religious Nonconformity to the man who was hard, narrow, and unimaginative; but it would suggest a policy of discriminating comprehension to one who could discriminate and sympathise. BANCROFT and BACON may stand as representatives of the two types. Unfortunately it was BANCROFT who 'called the tune' under JAMES I., not BACON.

This was the more unfortunate because Puritanism was being silently transformed from within, and for the better.

'The old Puritanism which had busied itself with caps and surplices, and with energetic protests against everything which bore the slightest resemblances to the practices of the Roman Church, was gradually dropping out of sight, and a movement was taking place which careless and prejudiced writers have attributed to the strictness of JAMES and BANCROFT,

but which was in reality derived from
a far higher source.   The fact was,
that thoughtful Englishmen were less
occupied in combating Spain and the
Pope, and more occupied in combating
immorality and sin than they had
been in the days of ELIZABETH.   .   .
A generation was arising of Puritan
conformists, who had ceased to trouble
themselves about many questions
which had seemed all-important to
their fathers.   They were not anxious
to see the now customary forms of the
Church of England give way to those
of Scotland or Geneva, and they were
ready to accept the Prayer Book as a
whole, even if they disliked some of
its expressions.   What they lost in
logic they gained in breadth.   They
desired that under the teaching of
the Bible, interpreted as it was by
them through the medium of the
Calvinist theology, every Englishman
should devote himself to the fulfil-

ment of those duties in which they
saw the worthy preparation for the
life to come. . . . It was by its
demand for a purer morality that
Puritanism retained its hold upon the
laity.' [1]

To this statement of Dr. GARDINER we
may add that of Dr. USSHER that 'the
Puritans of the Civil War were the growth
of the years succeeding 1615, and have
little more than a sort of historical connection with the earlier phases of the
movement.' [2]

The change in Puritanism is pointed
out by an anonymous verse-writer in a
political poem called 'The Interpreter,'
published in 1622 :—

'Time was, a PURITAN was counted such
  As held some Ceremonies were too much
  Retained and urged ; and would no Bishops grant,
  Others to rule, who government did want.'

---

[1] v. S. R. Gardiner, 'History of England,' iii. 239 f.
[2] 'Reconstruction of the English Church,' vol. i.
p. 256.

Now, a Puritan is the synonym for a genuine patriot, and hardly less for a devoutly religious man :—

'A PURITAN is he, that, twice a day,
  Doth at the least, to God devoutly pray,
  And twice a Sabbath, he goes to church to hear,
  To pray, confess his sins, and praise God there
  In open sight of all men : not content
  God knows his heart, except his knee be bent,
  That men, and angels likewise, may discern
  He came to practise there, as well as learn ;
  And honour God, with every outward part,
  With knee, hand, tongue, as well as with the heart.

The close of the sixteenth century witnessed a great increase in the wealth of the country.   While the continent was distracted and impoverished by the religious wars, England enjoyed domestic peace.   Trade passed from the cities of Germany and Belgium to Holland and England, and in the wake of trade came riches and luxury.   There was a rapid and alarming declension in public morals. The long struggle maintained against

Spain in the Netherlands told badly on the morality of the combatants, among whom must be reckoned large numbers of Englishmen, employed by the Queen, or fighting as volunteers against the arch-enemy of Protestantism. 'It hath been observed,' writes FULLER, 'that the sin of drunkenness was first brought over into England out of the Low Countries about the middle of the reign of Queen ELIZABETH.' Sir THOMAS OVERBURY, writing in 1609, says of the Dutch that 'they are given all to drink, and, eminently, to no other vice.' HEYLYN, in his 'Microcosmus,' published in 1625, says that the Netherlanders are 'much given to our English beer,' and adds that the Netherlands 'have in these late days been the Campus Martius, or School of Defence for all Christendom; to which the youth of all nations repair to see the manner of fortifications and learn the art of war.' [1]

[1] Pp. 227, 250.

'*Suffer not thy sons to pass the Alps,*' was one of the precepts which Lord BURLEIGH gave to his son, the first Earl of Salisbury, and he added as the reason that 'they would learn nothing there but pride, blasphemy, and atheism.' Lord BURLEIGH had to the full the Englishman's prejudice against all things foreign, but his severe estimate of Italian morals is fully borne out by other and unexceptionable evidence :—-

> ' I cannot easily resolve,' wrote BEDELL from Venice in 1608, 'whether this people be more deeply drowned in ignorance or sin; each, indeed, being the effect and cause of other ; both be so great, as if it be true, which is said, things mend when they are at the worst, it cannot in reason be far off, that God should by His judgment or mercy work some alteration.' [1]

' It [*i.e.,* Italian vice] is known suffi-

[1] v. 'Two Biographies of William Bedell,' p. 229.

ciently to all men,' wrote Sir EDWYN
SANDYS, in his famous ' Speculum Europæ,'
published anonymously in 1605, without the
author's consent, and by himself in 1613,

> 'and too much to some, who not
> content to sport themselves with all
> Italian impurities, proceed on to em-
> poison their country also at their return
> thither, that we need not marvel if
> those rarer villanies which our an-
> cestors never dreamed of, do now
> grow frequent, and such men whom
> they would have swept out of the
> street of their cities, as the noisom
> disgrace and dishonour of them, and
> confined to a dungeon or other deso-
> late habitation, do vaunt themselves
> now, and with no mean applause, for
> the only gallants and worthy spirits
> of the world.' [1]

There was much intercourse with the Continent, and men observed with disgust and

[1] v. 'Europæ Speculum,' p. 19.   London, 1673.

dismay the rehearsal in England of notions and fashions learned in Paris, Venice, and Rome.   It is impossible to understand the later Puritanism, unless the aggressiveness of foreign vice be borne in mind.   The serious mind of the nation was revolted by the licentiousness which was invading English society, and, if the National Church should fail adequately to interpret that mind, Puritanism would attain a strength and dignity which it had never yet attained.

James I. had many merits.   He was conscientious where his interest was engaged, industrious, really concerned for religion, fond of learned men, learned himself, possessed of no mean portion of Scottish astuteness, and genuinely devoted to peace.   Let me quote Dr. Gardiner's measured words as to his personal faults : they will indicate sufficiently the reason why the King failed to enlist the confidence, or command the respect, of his best subjects :—

' It was not only by living in an in
tellectual world of his own that JAMES
failed to gain a hold on the hearts
of Englishmen. The riotous profusion of his Court gave wide offence.
In July, 1606, when his brother-in-
law, CHRISTIAN IV. of Denmark,
visited him, ladies who were to act
in a dramatic performance before the
two kings were too drunk to play
their parts, and the offence was left
uncorrected. His own life was a
double one. He liked the company
of the learned, who could discuss with
him questions of theology and of
ecclesiastical politics, but he also liked
the boon companionship of the hunting
field ; and though his own life was
pure, and his own head, according to
his physician's report, too hard to be
affected by wine, he himself indulged
in coarse language, and took no pains
to avoid the society of evil livers.' [1]

[1] v. Dictionary of National Biography, xxix. 170.

The citadel of social corruption was the Court, and loyalty itself could not deny the fact, when the portentous scandal of Lady Essex's divorce, and the awful crime to which it led Lady Essex and her partner, Robert Carr, the reigning Favourite, exhibited the King's immediate entourage in a blaze of moral abomination. Puritanism is not understood until it be seen against this background of illustrious wickedness, in which the Supreme Governor of the Church appeared, on the most favourable view, as a weak and complaisant figure. James never allowed his regal position in the ecclesiastical system to be forgotten or belittled. From his first entrance into England he had taken the attitude of a religious partisan. His personal hostility to Puritanism had been already disclosed in his little treatise, 'Basilicon Doron,' written for his son's instruction in king-craft, and published in London during the very year of his accession to the English throne. 'Cherish no

man more than a good pastor,' he wrote,
' *hate no man more than a proud Puritan.*'
His dislike was as much political as religious : for as an intelligent despot, bent
on establishing his absolute authority, he
recognised in the Scottish Presbyters his
most formidable opponents. ' *Their con-
ceited parity,*' he said, ' *can neither stand
with the order of the Church, nor the peace
of a Common-weale and well-ruled Monarchy.*' In the Hampton Court Conference
he had carried himself in the chair as an
open partisan, and had wound up the
debates with the sinister threat that he
would ' *make the Puritans conform themselves, or harry them out of the land.*'
His phrase, which gave such delight to
the representatives of the Church, ' *No
Bishop, no King,*' gives the essence of
his ecclesiastical policy in a nutshell.
Hence the unfortunate association of the
episcopal case with hostility to the rising
standard of national righteousness. BAXTER
has left on record the impression made on

his boyish mind when he heard his father jeered at by the neighbours as a Puritan only for the strictness of his religious habit and the purity of his morals :—

'When I heard them call my father *Puritan* it did much to cure me and alienate me from them ; for I considered that my father's exercise of reading the Scripture was better than theirs, and would surely be better thought on by all men at the last, and I considered for what it was that he and others were thus derided. When I heard them speak scornfully of others as *Puritans* whom I never knew, I was at first apt to believe all the lies and slanders wherewith they loaded them ; but when I heard my own father so reproached, and perceived the drunkards were the forwardest in the reproach, I perceived that it was mere malice. For my father never scrupled

Common-prayer or Ceremonies, nor
spake against Bishops, nor ever so
much as prayed but by a book or
form, being not ever acquainted then
with any that did otherwise; but
only for reading Scripture when the
rest were dancing on the Lord's
Day, and for praying (by a Form out
of the end of the Common-prayer
Book) in his house, and for reprov-
ing drunkards and swearers, and for
talking sometimes a few words of
Scripture and the life to come, he was
reviled commonly by the name of
Puritan, Precisian, and Hypocrite;
and so were the godly conformable
ministers that lived anywhere in the
country near us, not only by our
neighbours, but by the common talk
of the vulgar rabble of all about us.
By this experience I was fully con-
vinced that Godly people were the
best, and those that despised them
and lived in sin and pleasure were a

malignant unhappy sort of people :
and this kept me out of their company, except now and then when the
love of sports and play enticed me.' [1]

When BAXTER was eighteen he went up
to London with the intention of making a
start in life. There he learned that the
revilers of his good father were more in
favour with the authorities of Church
and State than their victim :—

> ' I had quickly enough of the Court,'
> he says, ' when I saw a Stage-play
> instead of a Sermon on the Lord's
> Day in the afternoon, and saw what
> course was there in fashion, and
> heard little preaching, but what was
> as to one part against the Puritans,
> I was glad to be gone.' [2]

Mrs. HUTCHINSON, herself a strong
Puritan, writing of her father-in-law, Sir

[1] v. Life, pp. 2, 3.   [2] v. Life, p. 11.

THOMAS HUTCHINSON, describes a similar instance to that of BAXTER's father :—

> ' He was a man of a most moderate and wise spirit, but still so inclined to favour the oppressed saints and honest people of those times, that, though he conformed to the government, the licentious and profane encroachers upon common native rights branded him with *the reproach of the world, though the glory of good men—Puritanism*, yet notwithstanding he continued constant to the best interest, and died in London in the year 1643, a sitting member of that glorious Parliament that so generously attempted, and had almost affected, England's perfect liberty.' [1]

By some strange fatality JAMES fell out with the public conscience in all its more

[1] v. 'Memoirs of Col. Hutchinson,' ed. Firth, p. 33.

conspicuous expressions. Precisely at the moment when public opinion was becoming sensitive on the question of morals, his court was discredited by a monstrous scandal, and his own profusion was creating a financial crisis. Just when the moral reformation was linking itself to the movement for a stricter observance of the Lord's Day, he issued his rash though well-intentioned 'Book of Sports.' At a time when the minds of religious men were absorbed in the highly speculative controversies which grew from the Calvinistic theology, he issued (1622) his fatuous 'Directions concerning Preachers,' in which he limited to bishops and deans only the right 'to preach in any popular auditory the deep points of predestination, election, reprobation or of the universality, efficacity, resistibility or irresistibility of God's grace,' When the general mind of religious people accorded with the Puritan exaltation of preaching as the first and most important of the Christian minister's

duties, JAMES ordered that no parish
clergyman or lecturer should preach 'but
upon some part of the catechism, or some
text taken out of the Creed, Ten Com-
mandments, or the Lord's Prayer (funeral
sermons only excepted), and that those
preachers be most encouraged and approved of, who spend the afternoon's
exercise in the examining of children in
their catechism, and in the expounding of
the several points and heads of the catechism, which is the most ancient and
laudable custom of teaching in the Church
of England.' The whole of the Directions
was offensive to the Puritan ; the tone of
scarcely veiled contempt which ran
through them most of all. The self-
respect of religious men was wounded by
this direct interference of the monarch
with concerns which were manifestly outside the sphere of the State. It was
an affront to the Christian conscience.
Again, precisely at a time when the
national dread of all things Roman had

been rendered almost fanatical by the
Gunpowder Plot, and by the course of
events on the continent, JAMES entered
on his negotiations for the Spanish mar-
riage, and drew upon himself the sus-
picions of his people with respect to the
matter which most of all stirred them.
Consider the significance of five events
which happened in the year 1618: the
issue of the 'Book of Sports,' the execu-
tion of Sir WALTER RALEIGH, the beginning of the Thirty Years' War, the
meeting of the Synod of Dort, and the
attack on the Scottish Church at the
Assembly of Perth. The first alienated
the Sabbatarians, that is, all the more
serious Puritans; the next demonstrated
the king's ignoble deference to Spain; the
third disclosed the imminent peril of the
Protestant cause; the fourth reminded the
nation of its ancient intimacy with the
very protagonists of Protestantism; the
last showed the King making a crafty and
tyrannous attack on the Presbyterians of

his native land. Puritanism came to be almost synonymous with patriotism, and thus the great disadvantage, under which the earlier Puritans had laboured, was actually transferred to their opponents. The monarchy fell out of accord with the national mind, and stamped its own growing unpopularity on the Church, which it had bound so closely to itself.

Of course there was danger in the very intensity of the Puritan zeal for righteousness. As the conflict between the Puritans and their opponents developed, both sides were worsened by the exaggerated emphasis which they were led to place on their respective points of difference. 'Though,' writes Mr. FIRTH, 'the cause of the breach between the Stuarts and their people was more religious than political, religion and politics were almost inseparably associated in the struggle from its origin to its close. In practice it was found that men who held a certain set of views about Church affairs held an equally definite set of views about State affairs, and that there was a definite connection between their political and their religious creeds.'[1]

Men were drawn into the profession of Puritanism by mixed motives : here a zeal for righteousness predominated, and there a dislike of LAUD's ceremonial innovations, and there again a passion for political liberty, and there a reasoned belief in Presbyterianism. As the political blunders of the kings, and their financial extravagance, brought general odium on the government, so Puritanism came into the perilous situation of being actually popular with large sections of the population. The affectation of Puritan enthusiasm had an obvious political value, and seemed but a small price to pay for popularity to many unscrupulous politicians. '*Corruptio optimi pessima,*' is a saying which nowhere finds more striking illustration than in the history

[1] v. 'Stuart Tracts,' p. xiii.

of spiritual movements, which in their
exaltation have disdained the common
safeguards of system, or in their zeal
have exaggerated system into an impossible burden. Puritanism has exhibited both types of failure.

The 'Nonconformist Conscience' was
more potent and not less questionable
in the seventeenth century than in the
twentieth, but it had in the earlier
period one safeguard against hypocrisy
which it has long ceased to possess—
its expression was commonly conditioned
by personal sacrifice. Mainly, indeed,
in both centuries it was a sincere and
noble force, seeking for righteousness
and working it; but often, too often, it
was neither sincere nor noble, only a
profitable convention. Then and now
its bane was politics. The degradation
of Puritanism was latent in its association,
natural, indeed, and perhaps in the circumstances inevitable, with one of the
great parties in the conflict between

King and Parliament, in which both parties enjoyed and abused a brief triumph, and from which emerged finally that political compromise which we were once accustomed to boast of as 'the British Constitution.' It is not necessary to draw on the prejudiced and extravagant denunciations of their opponents in order to find the evidence of widespread hypocrisy among the Puritans of the seventeenth century. The wisest of the Puritan leaders perceived and deplored the fact; and the final overthrow of political Puritanism was less due to the efforts of its foes than to the intolerable abuses which attached to its rule. It will be worth while to refer to one representative authority.

A candid and eminent Puritan, SAMUEL TORSHELL, in his excellent treatise, 'The Hypocrite Discovered and Cured,' published in 1644, with an Epistle to the Assembly of Divines, illustrates his thesis with portraits evidently drawn from life.

'One man,' he says, 'would sometimes pleasantly tell his very private friends that he could buy commodities the cheaper in the Exchange, because of his short hair and very little band.'[1] Such men were as unstable in their principles as they were extreme in their professions. 'I knew one man,' says TORSHELL, 'who set out like Jehu against corruptions, and overran even good manners, in some houses that entertained him, so that he would tear and deface any devotional picture (as they call it) wheresoever he came; and out of his detestation of Images would scarce endure a cross in a Gentleman's coat-of-arms; who afterwards, when a favourable Prebend wind had cooled him, came to be active for superstitious innovations, and of a bitter spirit against the godly minded.'[2] He quotes the phrase of ERASMUS about similar impostors in his day. They were *Evangeliophori*, Gospel-carriers,

[1] P. 14.   [2] P. 13.

Bible-hearers only. ' I cast not this title upon godly persons, as profane men do in scorn and derision of their necessary and commendable profession. But if any man obey not that word which he hears and talks of, but lives dissolutely, then I say to him, as he in ERASMUS, *Quid Polyphemo cum Evangelio?* What hath a lewd wicked man to do with the Gospel? And as he observes, many carry their Bibles, as the Franciscans hang the rule of their order at their girdles, but mind not to observe it : they take care to adorn their Bibles, to gild and string them richly, but no care that the Bible shall adorn their hearts. He tells us pleasantly of the Soldier that beat a blasphemer with his Bible, and so defended the Gospel with the Gospel, and broke his pate with it : and yet for all his zeal was noway such a man as the Gospel requires. Such are profane defenders of the Reformed Religion, yet are no way reformed. They will storm

against the Papists if they blemish our
Religion, and yet themselves never regard
the very rules of Christianity.'[1] There
were wise Puritan leaders who observed
the ostentation of oddity which many
Puritans affected with alarm :—

'Grace is a commanding thing, and
will have sober hair and sober
garments.—Yet an affected outside
is commonly suspicious. I once
persuaded a good woman to leave
off a singular dress, when I told
her we must live like sincere
Christians, but must go dressed like
our neighbours. It becomes no man
to have a speaking habit, it wins
nothing to God, it exposeth the
Godly often to derision. Wear your
band and your hat, and anything
else, as others do, so they be not
exorbitant. Ye have enough beside
to make ye known what ye are,

[1] P. 38.

namely, to let all that converse with you find that ye are holy and just and honest in all dealings. Let that speak us, rather than our coats.' [1]

From dress he passes to 'the affected tone that some use to speak in.' 'I was much taken,' he says,

> 'with the wit and fine spirit of a Godly Gentlewoman, and zealously affected in religion, who when her chaplain returning from London, where he had never been before, began to use and take up a whining fashion of speaking, she presently admonished him, *To live like a good man, but to speak like a man.*' [2]

It must be obvious that a man so sane and sensible as TORSHELL was the very type of a sound National Churchman. What was it that could make him an avowed opponent of the Established

[1] P. 15.   [2] P. 16.

System? We may conclude this lecture with reading the account which he himself has given of the process in his 'Epistle Dedicatory' to the Westminster Assembly, which was holding its sessions in the Jerusalem Chamber when he published the delightful and edifying treatise from which I have been quoting.

After urging the Assembly to 'remove every burden which the tyranny of abused Episcopacy had laid upon us,' he proceeds :—

> 'I call their courses *tyranny* and their Impositions *burthens*, as having had through the happiness of these late times better means and opportunities to discern and weigh them ; for let me speak freely, and as becomes us now that the hand of God is so much out against the nation, let me speak humbly, I confess my thoughts were heretofore more favourable, as walking according

to those principles I had received in my education. The truth is, though I never thought Episcopacy to be of Divine right, as it was proudly challenged, yet I looked upon it as the most ancient and most prudent way of government, and so obeyed it and spake well of it, though not its mad and furious ways, for I ever protested against their Altars and their *cringes*, their suppressing of faithful and painful preachers, their discouraging and undermining of the power of godliness, their wanton and profane abuse of the high and dreadful censure of excommunication ; yet in a general conformity to such things as I conceived were by law established, I obeyed it, as thinking it to be a sin not to have done so.   I will not be ashamed to put these charitable thoughts I had (for so I will call them, and so my own conscience, after I examined it, doth call them) among the *errata* of my life.'

A policy which could alienate from the National System such men as SAMUEL TORSHELL is self-condemned of fatuity.

THE INTELLECTUAL FAILURE
OF PURITANISM

III

THE INTELLECTUAL FAILURE OF PURITANISM

AS a moral protest against social corruption Puritanism commended itself to the general conscience. As the religious principle of the popular resistance to the autocratic system, which CHARLES and LAUD embodied, Puritanism gained the acceptance of the most virile sections of the people. But it failed to satisfy the intellectual needs of an age of eager questioning and progressive thought. It has left a vast literature of homiletics and casuistry, which is wholly dead save for an occasional excursion of the curious. Nothing could be more wearisome to the modern reader than its voluminous controversy. Its exegesis is illumined by many gleams of spiritual insight, but is everywhere spoiled by a slavish literalism, and an excessive deference to the authority of the great Protestant School-men. A few devotional treatises have survived, and even taken rank as spiritual classics; and two imaginative works of the first quality, 'Paradise Lost' and 'The Pilgrim's Progress,' belong to the choicest treasures of English literature. Puritan scholarship is nobly exhibited in the learned works of USSHER and LIGHT-FOOT; and Puritan political philosophy is well represented by the prose writings of MILTON and the 'Holy Common-wealth' of BAXTER. These compositions of genius, learning, and political thought, however, albeit coloured by the religious convictions of the authors, can hardly be regarded as properly illustrative of Puri-tanism. At least the connection must be held to be indirect, the contribution of a tone and the suggestion of a theme, rather than the inspiration of new ideas or the gift of new methods. Neither the science, nor the politics, nor the literature, nor the theology of the generation which had sat at the feet of the Puritans, and witnessed their brief triumph, was destined to develop on their principles. They would leave a powerful, and in the main a salutary, influence on the temper and habits of the people, but not on its thought. The Calvinistic theology, which was the intellectual form of Puritanism, is dead beyond recall. The attitude of unquestioning and literal acceptance which determined the Puritan's handling of the Bible, and made it for him a sufficient directory of conduct in all situations, has passed for ever. His view of the Roman Church may linger as the woeful eccentricity of individuals of pinched culture and unfortunate experience, but it can never again become the secure postulate of any considerable number of Christian people. Puritanism, as a coherent system of thought and life, belongs to the antiquities of English religion. It was showing unmistakable signs of obsoleteness in the very age which it dominated.

It is difficult for us to realise the absolute intellectual sovereignty, which was generally yielded to CALVIN in this country in the early decades of the seventeenth century. The note of revolt, however, had already been sounded. The first four books of HOOKER's 'Ecclesiastical Polity' were published in 1594, and they included a grave protest against the excessive deference which English Churchmen were wont to exhibit to the great French doctor. HOOKER's language is restrained and discriminating, but it is none the less decisive :—

'Two things of principal moment there are which have deservedly procured him [CALVIN] honour through-

out the world : the one his exceeding
pains in composing the " Institutions
of Christian Religion " : the other his
not less industrious travails for exposition of holy Scripture according
unto the same Institutions. In which
two things whosoever they were that
after him bestowed their labour, he
gained the advantage of prejudice
against them, if they gainsayed ; and of
glory above them, if they consented.
His writings published after the question about that discipline was once
begun, omit not any the least
occasion of extolling the use and
singular necessity thereof. Of what
account the Master of Sentences was
in the Church of Rome, the same and
more amongst the preachers of
reformed churches CALVIN has pur-
chased : so that the perfectest divines
were judged they, which were skil-
fullest in CALVIN'S writings. His
books almost the very canon to judge

both doctrine and discipline by. French churches, both under others abroad and at home in their own country, all cast according to that mould which CALVIN had made. The church of Scotland, in erecting the fabric of their reformation, took the self-same pattern. Till at length the discipline, which was at first so weak, that without the staff of their approbation, who were not subject unto it themselves, it had not brought others under subjection, began now to challenge universal obedience, and to enter into open conflict with those very churches which in desperate extremity had been relievers of it.' [1]

SANDERSON relates that when he was a student at Oxford about the year 1608, CALVIN'S ' Institutions' were commended to the students ' as the best and perfectest system of Divinity, and fittest to be laid as

[1] v. ' Eccl. Pol.,' Preface ii. 8.

a groundwork in the study of that profession.' He himself was favourably impressed by it :—

> ' I found, so far as I was then able to
> judge, the method exact, the expres-
> sions clear, the style grave, equal, and
> unaffected, his doctrine for the most
> part conform to St. Augustine's, in a
> word, the whole work very elaborate,
> and useful to the Churches of God in
> a good measure ; and might have
> been, I verily believe, much more
> useful, if the honour of his name had
> not given so much reputation to his
> very errors. I must acknowledge
> myself to have reaped great benefit
> by the reading thereof.' [1]

Calvinism owes its modern reputation
less to its principles than to the system of
morality and polity which were based on
them, and to the circumstances in which

[1] v. Works, ed. Jacobson, vol. v. 297 f.

they were advocated. CALVIN's main
principle—the unflinching assertion of
Divine sovereignty in religion—was
not original. As Bishop SANDERSON
justly observed, 'his doctrine was for the
most part conform to St. Augustine's,'
and ST. AUGUSTINE drew it from the
writings of ST. PAUL. Accordingly there
was no essential connection between
CALVIN's doctrine and his ecclesiastical
polity, and in point of fact the first was
accepted by those, like the illustrious
USSHER, who rejected the last. Between
ST. AUGUSTINE and CALVIN, moreover,
there were some crucial differences. The
great Latin Father wrote from within the
historic Catholic Church, and as its
spokesman : the French divine wrote
from without the historic Church, and as
its antagonist. The one sought and found
the application of his religious theory
within the established sacramental system,
which in his day was theoretically un-
challenged and practically almost co-

extensive with the Christian profession. The other was forced to reject the traditional organisation of Christendom, and to discover another sphere within which his dogmatic scheme might be realized. St. Augustine accepted the established ecclesiastical system, and argued from it: Calvin rejected the established polity, and framed an alternative. Both built on the Scriptures, but with a difference. St. Augustine read them as the first and governing utterance of the inspired Society of the visible Catholic Church: Calvin read them as an independent authority, which, in the actual circumstances of an apostate Church, was a hostile authority. There was nothing in the situation of the older Thinker which can be paralleled with the desperate circumstances in which the Founder of Calvinism fashioned a fighting creed for the Protestant world The strength and the weakness of Calvinism lay in the fact that it was a fighting creed.

It raised the Infallible Book against the Infallible Church : the sure guarantee of an 'effectual calling' against the external pledge of a valid sacrament : the dynamic force of individual conviction against the corporate strength of immemorial orthodoxy. It was clear in its premisses, inexorable in its logic, remorseless in its conclusions. It was a creed for soldiers, and its most congenial circumstances were those of the stricken field. Its supreme exponents were soldiers—WILLIAM THE SILENT, Admiral COLIGNY, OLIVER CROMWELL, GUSTAVUS ADOLPHUS, countless others of equal faith though lesser name, who in the might of their Calvinistic creed rolled back the tide of the Counter-Reformation, broke the spell of Jesuit subtlety, and saved the liberties of Europe.

But the fighting qualities of Calvinism militated against it in time of peace. The Bible could not permanently sustain the character which Calvinism imposed on it.

The attitude of immitigable hatred against
the Roman Church could not be maintained when the excitements of conflict
had ceased, and men considered the issues
between the Churches as students, and
fellow-Christians, rather than as mortal
antagonists. The iconoclastic fervour,
which went well enough with the desperate situation of men fighting against
great odds for all that they hold most
dear, seemed excessive and even absurd
when they continued to profess the old
immitigable sentiments, and to use the old
ferocious language in time of peace.
Leisure advanced claims of its own. The
æsthetic faculties, submerged and forgotten in the time of conflict, began to assert
themselves insistently in a more normal
and settled age. The intellect, which had
been absorbed in the immediate concerns
of war, developed a new independence so
soon as peace lifted the obsession of a
great fear from the human mind, and
gave it liberty of self-expression. The

artist, the scholar, the man of science, the man of devotion, the ordinary citizen—each and all had a grievance against the dour, unyielding system which had seemed self-evidently true in the earlier time of stress. After the confusions of the religious crisis, peace was first attained in England, and there-fore in England the reaction against the system of Calvinism began early, and rapidly developed. First, as was natural, the Presbyterian polity, which had become associated with CALVIN's doctrinal scheme, was definitely rejected. At a later period, indeed, when the Civil War was in pro-gress, the Puritans were driven by their military weakness to purchase the support of the Scots at the price of subscribing the 'Solemn League and Covenant,' but the Presbyterian polity, which was thereby bound on the nation, had no strength in popular regard, flourished nowhere, and sank quickly under the rising tide of sec-tarianism, and, when that in turn had ebbed, under the stronger tide of constitutionalism in Church and State. The revolt against the dogmatic system of CALVIN was slower in development, but not less complete in its ultimate victory. It had already begun while ELIZABETH was yet on the throne. It made rapid way under her successors.

The revolt against doctrinal Calvinism broke out first where it might have been expected to break out—in the Universities. Cambridge, like Oxford 250 years later, was the scene of a 'movement,' which, after being temporarily crushed in the place of its birth, spread quickly in the country, and finally triumphed everywhere. Both movements began in a University sermon. On April 29, 1595, WILLIAM BARRET, a young Fellow of Gonville and Caius College, created a sensation by a *Concio ad Clerum*, delivered in the University Church for his B.D. degree. The Vice-Chancellor, giving expression to the general indignation, peremptorily insisted on a public recantation, but this, when at length the offender was induced to make it, only added fuel to the fire. A considerable number of Fellows of Colleges set their hands to a protest, in which they stated with considerable vigour their opinion on Mr. BARRET'S performances :—

'We do declare,' they said, 'first, touching the said Sermon that in our judgments and consciences, it was very corrupt, savouring of Popish doctrine in the whole course and tenour thereof (even as the Popish writers do maintain) interlaced with contumelious and bitter speeches against the chief, godly, learned, new writers, as PETER MARTYR, CALVIN, BEZA, ZANCHIUS, &c., who are worthily received and reverenced in our Church. And finally so strange and offensive both to us . and all others of sound religion in our University, as we never heard the

like preached in Cambridge, or elsewhere, since the beginning of her
Majesty's most gracious reign. And
for his Retractation (being done and
read in a very unreverend, profane,
and impudent manner) it rather added
new offence and grief of heart unto
us, and many other, than any satisfaction of the former, so as we hope
there will be further order taken with
him, for better satisfying so publick
and just offence.'[1]

Both sides now appealed to the Archbishop. BARRET at first gained some
advantage, for WHITGIFT was annoyed at
the hasty action of the academic authorities, not altogether pleased with their zeal
for the foreign divines, whose authority
had been too often pleaded by the Puritans
against the ceremonial system for him to
regard them without suspicion, and very
much annoyed at the slight respect which

[1] v. Strype, "Whitgift," bk. iv. 436.

had been shown to his own authority.
' To traduce CALVIN and other learned
men in pulpits—he said—he could by no
means like. Neither did he allow the
same towards AUGUSTINE, JEROME, and
other learned Fathers. Which nevertheless had often and many times been
abused in the University without control.
And yet if a man would have occasion to
control Calvin for his bad and unchristian
censure of K. HENRY VIII., or him and
others, in that peremptory and false
reproof of this Church of England in
divers points, and likewise in some other
singularities, he knew no Article of
Religion against it. Much less did he
know any cause, why men should be so
violently dealt withal for it : or termed
ungodly, Popish, impudent. For the
doctrine of the Church of England did
in no respect depend upon them.' [1]

The conflict in Cambridge was confused
by local issues ; but it illustrates the

[1] v. Strype, iv. 441.

general situation. In order to assuage the controversy, which was beginning to endanger the discipline of the University, the Archbishop finally issued the nine dogmatic decisions, which are known as the *Lambeth Articles.* These are strongly Calvinistic, although they seem to have been designed as an Eirenicon. Incidentally they led to a recrudescence of the strife in Cambridge, for PETER BARO, the Margaret Professor of Divinity, a learned Frenchman who was known to dislike CALVIN's views, took the Lambeth Articles for the subject of a sermon, on January 12, 1596, 'in which he moderated, and stated, as he apprehended, the true sense of them.' WHITGIFT expressed himself in terms of much irritation, and the Queen, always sensitive to the risks of theological controversy, was highly incensed. In the event, the Lambeth Articles were suffered to drop, and PETER BARO lost his professorship.

Meanwhile the Calvinistic Theology

maintained its supremacy, and was strengthened by the change of dynasty. For the new monarch from Scotland was himself a strong Calvinist, and interested himself keenly in his partisan way in the controversy which distracted the Netherlands. In this, as in so many other respects, JAMES exhibited a paradoxical aspect, almost unintelligible to his subjects. Thus he sent a deputation of eminent English prelates to DORT, where the Arminians were put down with a high hand, but at home he was surrounded by Arminian ecclesiastics, and filled the bishopricks and deaneries with them. The key to his contradictions lay in his despotism. As he hated the Puritans in spite of their Calvinism, because they opposed his autocratic tendencies, so he favoured the Arminians in spite of their Arminianism, because they fell in with his political methods. His appointment of ABBOTT as Archbishop of Canterbury, in succession to BANCROFT, was, indeed, a notable triumph for Calvinism, but the current ran ever more strongly against it in the Universities and among the clergy : and when both JAMES and ABBOTT had passed away, their places were taken by those whose sympathies were wholly with the new doctrines.

Meanwhile the standing controversy with Rome had entered on a new phase since the Jesuits had gained the mastery of the papal policy, which they have generally succeeded in retaining ever since. Hitherto the Protestants had been clearly superior to their opponents along the whole line of attack. They were the best preachers, the clearest thinkers, the ablest writers, the most acceptable moralists of the time. In every form of conflict the representatives of the unreformed Medieval Church were outclassed and defeated. But now the tide was visibly turning. The Roman Church had purged itself of its most embarrassing scandals : it was or-ganised for aggressive warfare, and could bring into the field superior numbers of well-trained, strictly-disciplined, enthusiastic combatants. Sir EDWYN SANDYS, writing at the close of the sixteenth century, comments with much acuteness on the change which he perceived to be taking place. His description is strictly contemporary, and drawn from personal observation. He tells us that the Romanists had copied the methods of their opponents so successfully, that now at every point the Protestants were in danger of being beaten on their own ground, and with their own weapons. The Jesuits, he says, had 'attained the commendation and worked the effect of as perfect orators as those times did yield'; that in publishing 'Books of Prayer and Piety' they had 'so surpassed their opposites, that they forbore not to reproach unto them their poverty, weakness, and coldness in that kind, as being forced to take the Catholicks' Books to supply therein'; that they now feared no longer those public disputations in which Protestants had commonly gained so great advantage, but even found it profitable themselves to invite such encounters; above all, that they made their own the whole range of education, especially laying themselves out to gain control over well-born children who were likely to wield influence in later life. ' In all places wherever they can plant their nests, they open Free Schools for all studies of Humanity. To these flock the best wits, the principal men's sons, in so great abundance that wherever they settle, other colleges become desolate, or frequented only by the baser sort, and of heavier metal; and in truth, such is their diligence and dexterity in instructing, that even the Protestants in some places send their sons unto their schools, upon desire to have them prove excellent in those arts they teach. . . . This point of their Schools and instructing Youth is thought of such moment by men of wisdom and judgment, being taught so by very experience and trial thereof, that the planting of a good College of Jesuits in any place, is esteemed the only sure way to replant that Religion, and in time to eat out the contrary.'[1]

Now the Puritans with their Calvinistic theology, their rigid literalism, their irrational Sabbatarianism, their ruthless iconoclasm, and their contempt for the traditions and usages of historical Christianity, were ill suited for the controversy which the Jesuits invited. If moral fervour and strength of personal conviction could ever take the place of knowledge and skill, they would have been as irresistible in the field of polemical warfare as in that of hard fighting, but since this can never be, they fell into the background, and ceased to command the respect of the intellectual class. In this connection we may refer to the abortive scheme for establishing a college — 'King JAMES's College in Chelsea '—'for a spiritual garrison, with

[1] v. Survey, pp. 84, 85, 90, 93.

a magazine of all books for that purpose, where learned divines should study and write in maintenance of all controversies against the papists.' In relating the failure of this pretentious and ill-designed project, FULLER allows the polemical superiority of the Roman Catholics, and suggests as the reason the parochial distractions of the Anglican champions, which disqualified them for conflict with opponents who were experts in the polemical art :—

'The Romish church doth not burden their professors with preaching, or any parochial incumbrances, but reserves them only for polemical studies. Whereas in England the same man reads, preacheth, catechiseth, disputes, delivers sacraments, &c. So that, were it not for God's marvellous blessing on our studies, and the infinite odds of truth on our sides, it were impossible, in human probability, that we should hold up the bucklers against them.'

Of course, there is some truth in this, but it omits the main disqualification under which the Protestant controversialists laboured—their Calvinistic Creed. In 1610 an illustrious scholar, ISAAC CASAUBON, whose monument is not the least interesting in this Abbey Church, sought the hospitality of these shores. He was flying from Calvinistic narrowness, almost as much as from Romanist cruelty. His brilliant modern biographer, MARK PATTISON, in relating the reasons which led him to take refuge in England, makes some illuminating observations on the situation in this country. He points out that the Huguenot scholar had been rendered dissatisfied with Calvinism by 'the necessity of daily encountering the catholic disputants.'

'The ministers of his own communion scouted antiquity, of which

they were ignorant, and which CASAU-
BON regarded as the only arbiter of
the quarrel. Books fell in his way
written on this side of the channel,
in which he met with a line of
argument very different from the
uninstructed, but presumptuous dog-
matism of the calvinist ministers.
He found to his surprise and delight
that there were others beside himself
who could respect the authority of
the fathers, without surrendering
their reason to the dicta of the papal
church. The young anglo-catholic
school which was then forming in
England took precisely the ground
which CASAUBON had been led to
take against DU PERRON.

'.The change of face which English theology effected in the reign of
JAMES I. is, to our generation, one
of the best known facts in the history
of our church. But it is often taken
for granted that this revolution was

brought about by the ascendancy of one man, whose name is often used to denominate the school as the Laudian school of divines. LAUD was the political leader, but in this capacity only the agent of a mode of thinking which he did not invent. Anglo-catholic theology is not a system of which any individual thinker can claim the invention. It arose necessarily, or by natural development, out of the controversy with the papal advocates, as soon as that controversy was brought out of the domain of pure reason into that of learning. That this peculiar compromise, or *via media*, between Romanism and Calvinism developed itself in England, and nowhere else in Christendom, is owing to causes which this is not the place to investigate. But that it was a product not of English soil, but of theological learning wherever sufficient learning existed, is evidenced by the history of CASAUBON'S mind, who now found himself in 1610, an anglican ready made, as the mere effect of reading the fathers to meet DU PERRON'S incessant attacks.'[1]

Learning, then, especially the learning which was required for controversy with the Romanist, would not make a man a Puritan. The exemption from the religious wars which the island kingdom enjoyed, and the comparative wealth of the island Church, brought the controversial weakness of Calvinism into prominence, and fostered the growth of a learned type of Protestantism.

Lack of learning was a grave fault, but far graver was contempt for human reason, and the Puritans, in the bondage of their Calvinistic creed, lay exposed to this charge also. Already the finest minds were reacting against the ferocity

[1] v. 'Isaac Casaubon,' pp. 299, 300.

and futility of incessant controversies
between churches, and were seeking a
footing for faith apart from the authority
of fathers, churches, and systems. In
the calm reasoning of RICHARD HOOKER
there was latent the developed argument
of CHILLINGWORTH. Both made their
appeal to the human spirit itself, ultimate
judge of the sense of Scripture, and
clothed with a higher and nearer authority
than any external power could vindicate.
CHEYNELL was a bitter and violent
Puritan, and the curious tract in which
he narrates the death and burial of
WILLIAM CHILLINGWORTH may be interpreted as a proof that his treatment of
that illustrious man was felt generally
to have been discreditably harsh. Yet
he gave expression to the general view
of Puritans as to CHILLINGWORTH's teaching, when he hurled the ' Religion of
Protestants ' into its author's grave, and
accompanied his action with words of
vehement denunciation. ' Remember,'

he wrote in his Prefactory Letter to 'the Friends of Mr. CHILLINGWORTH,' 'that your friend did run mad with reason, and so lost his reason and religion both at once ; he thought he might trust his reason in the highest points ; his reason was to be judge, whether or no there be a God ? Whether that God wrote any Book ? Whether the Books usually received as Canonical be the Books, the Scriptures of God ? What is the sense of those Books ? What Religion is best ? What Church purest ? ' Posterity has passed its verdict on the two men. The liberal Anglican has taken his place, a great place, among the Masters of religious thought ; the Puritan only lives by virtue of his connection with his victim.

In the wake of the new rationalism came a perception of the outrage and folly of persecution. But Puritanism, fettered by its prejudices, set itself against toleration. Holding Roman Catholics to be 'idolators,' and finding in the Old Testament that idolatry was Divinely ordered to be punished by death, the Puritan was always restless at any approach to a tolerant treatment of his Romanist fellow-citizens. His intolerance was not confined to the treatment of Roman Catholics. Archbishop ABBOT, a strong Puritan, pressed for the burning of the unhappy sectaries, LEGATT and WIGHTMAN, who perished at the stake in 1612. The Puritans marked their temporary supremacy by the cruel persecution of those whom the superstition of the age accounted to be witches; and when, in America, they had a free hand, they treated the Quakers with abominable cruelty. No doubt the age was intolerant, and save for an oppressed sectary here and there, the notion of religious toleration was scouted. Still, it cannot be denied that the Puritans made a conscience of intolerance when others were moving towards more humane positions.

ROGER WILLIAMS, the sectary, WILLIAM CHILLINGWORTH, the Latitudinarian, JEREMY TAYLOR, the High Churchman, —all these were leaders in the march from bigotry to humaneness, and none of them was a Puritan.

The intellectual failure of Puritanism, then, cannot be questioned. Had not CHARLES and LAUD forced political issues to the front, and bound up their own religious views with a political system which menaced English liberty, the failure of the Puritans would have been sooner perceived. In point of fact, the political crisis gave a new lease of life to Puritanism, and postponed its defeat for a generation.

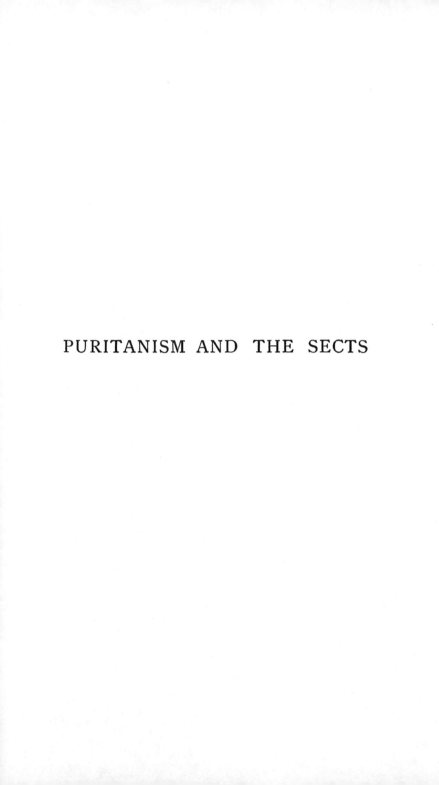

PURITANISM AND THE SECTS

IV

PURITANISM AND THE SECTS

THE Puritans were not dissenters, but they facilitated the process by which discontent with the established system passed into open separation from the Established Church. In modern times we have become so familiar with the fact of religious separation, expressing itself freely in autonomous sects, that we find it difficult to understand the extreme reluctance with which men, whose principles might seem to demand separation from the Church, yet regarded the notion of formal severance. Nothing, however, is more certain than that the Puritans condemned religious dissent, and scrupled not to exert themselves to suppress dissenters when they had power to do so. The 'sectaries' or 'schismaticks' were hardly less abhorrent to them than the 'papists,' and their sentiments were cordially reciprocated by those of whom they were both the teachers and the opponents.

If we examine closely the circumstances in which religious dissent arose in this country, we can hardly be surprised either at the fact itself, or at the peculiar form it received. The Reformation had both stimulated religious individualism, and weakened the ecclesiastical system which was its normal check. We do not sufficiently allow for either of these salient facts. Persecution is a wonderful tonic of character, and strengthens even while it misleads men. It is significant that the first beginnings of organised dissent in this country are traceable to the evil days of the Marian persecution. Then, in the teeth of desperate risks, and in plain defiance of the law, a congregation of Protestants had been formed in London, in order to continue the worship which had been established by EDWARD VI. To this separatist church, which used the prescribed Prayer-book, and kept the torch of Reformed Religion burning during the night of popish supremacy, the later sectaries looked back as a precedent for their own action, which their Anglican adversaries could not gainsay. Its justification lay in the fact, which no Puritan would dispute, that the medieval Church was apostate, and therefore that no religious validity attached to its ministry. Even Anglicans, like the learned and bigoted HEYLYN, could not condemn the Protestant dissenters who rejected the religious authority of Bishop BONNER; and yet such rejection logically implied both an attitude towards the medieval hierarchy, which was inconsistent with HEYLYN's churchmanship, and a resistance to the civil authority which could by no means be reconciled with the Anglican doctrine of the Royal Supremacy. The dissenting Protestants, indeed, were themselves quite unconscious of anything schismatical in their situation. They accounted that they alone represented the true Church of England, and that their diocesan, Bishop BONNER, was quite manifestly a tool of Antichrist. So indisputable in those days did the apostasy of the Roman Church appear, that there seemed no absurdity in clothing a congregation of a few score separatists with the character of a National Church. In truth there was little consistency in the religious world of that age of crisis. Principles and precedents were so many weapons of polemical warfare, used as occasion required, and repudiated readily enough when the occasion had passed.

The Established Church lent itself to effective apology on paper; but as a

working system it was deplorably open
to criticism.   It had no roots in popular
sentiment strong enough to sustain an
enforcement of its claims, and no adequate
efficiency to commend its arrangements.
The Reformation worked a revolution in
the minds of men not less violent than in
the institutions of religion.   Thus the
tradition of sacramental worship, together
with the mental dispositions and personal
disciplines which it presupposed, was
finally destroyed.   Religious Englishmen,
as a body, would never again respond to
the distinctive notes of the medieval
Church.   With the monasteries there
passed away the ascetic ideals and disciplines which the monasteries embodied
and symbolised.   With the Mass and the
Confessional vanished the sacerdotal
power and sacramental religion which had
found in these their most imposing expression, and their most effective instrument.
With the papacy went from English
minds the notion of Catholic Unity in

the old sense. The ecclesiastical system, which survived the great ruin, retained, indeed, the old political framework so far as it was not inconsistent with the royal autocracy; it preserved with jealous care the legal forms which guaranteed that formal continuity on which lawyers lay stress, and which statesmen recognise as important. But, to adapt a famous phrase, the new system was as the ghost of the medieval church sitting discrowned on the ruins thereof. In its weakness the Established Church leaned on the monarchy. The Privy Council took over, as an Ecclesiastical Commission, the functions of government which the bishops had no power to fulfil. Mr. USSHER has shown that ' The Reconstruction of the English Church ' was carried through by WHITGIFT and BANCROFT through the direct action of the State authority.

Puritans, generally, as we have shown in the previous lectures, were reconciled to the Established System during the latter years of ELIZABETH's reign, and set themselves to the supreme work of restoring religion and morality to the nation, which seemed in danger of losing both. But, when we examine carefully the presuppositions of this strong and even enthusiastic Puritan churchmanship, we can see that it had no promise of permanence. It acquiesced in a system which it could not approve, because, at the time, that system seemed plainly serviceable to the cause of religion, but, if this circumstance should cease, and loyalty to the system should be required from men whose convictions were plainly in conflict with its apparent tendency, it is clear that a situation would have arisen in which Puritanism would perforce change its aspect. The influence of the Bible, now widely read in the Genevan Version, began to tell in many directions. Its effect was in many respects favourable to the Established Church. The parallel

between the English nation and the
People of Israel, which was generally
drawn, and seems to have established
itself in the public mind almost as a
postulate, confirmed that intimate association of Church and State which was the
cornerstone of the Elizabethan Establishment. It would appear that the Old
Testament was more widely read than
the New, certainly its spirit rather than
that of the Christian Scriptures coloured
the religious thought of the nation. The
course of events on the continent, where
the Counter-Reformation seemed to be
threatening a total destruction of the
Reformed Churches, strengthened in
English minds the notion that the English people held a special position in the
providential scheme of history analogous
to that held by the ancient Israelites.
This notion was eminently congruous
with the prevailing Calvinism, which
suggested the idea of Divine Election
as belonging to the privileged and faith-

ful nation. Above all, Englishmen found in the astonishing facts of their own recent history a reason for believing that they were under the special protection of the ALMIGHTY. Such an idea is repulsive to the modern mind, as savouring of an intolerable vanity, and generally indicating a portentous ignorance. But neither vanity nor ignorance could be connected with it in that age. England had attained to such a pinnacle of prosperity and fame under ELIZABETH, that she was regarded with as much envy abroad as exultation at home. The Old Testament authenticated the belief that temporal blessings were proofs of Divine approbation. Accordingly we find that the prosperity of the country was boldly offered in evidence of the truth of its religion. A single example will sufficiently illustrate this frame of mind. In the year 1624, CARLETON, Bishop of Chichester, published his 'Thankful Remembrance of GOD's Mercy in an Historical Collection

of the great and merciful Deliverances of
the Church and State of England, since
the Gospel began here to flourish, from
the beginning of Queen ELIZABETH.' It
ran through several editions, and may be
taken as a fair exposition of the religious
Englishmen's views in the reign of JAMES I.
The thesis which the book maintains,
and illustrates from the history of England since the accession of ELIZABETH, is
that 'true religion bringeth a blessing,
and that religion that bringeth always a
curse is to be suspected.'[1] ELIZABETH, he
shows, had been uniformly successful ;
her adversaries as uniformly unfortunate.
'We see,' he says, 'GOD hath made our
enemies His enemies : they cannot fight
against us, but they must fight against
GOD, how much then are we bound to
honour and serve this great GOD of
heaven and earth that hath showed
such favour to His Church in England.'[2]
'My purpose in writing this book is to

[1] P. 26.   [2] P. 58.

declare the great works of GOD in the
defence of this Church of England since
Religion was planted here by Queen
ELIZABETH.' [1] He lays it down that it
is the privilege of the true Church of
GOD to enjoy a 'miraculous protection
and strange deliverance out of dangers.'
The Roman Church, he argues, is proved
to be forsaken of GOD by the uniform
failure of all its attempts against England,
and by the immoral methods which it
never scrupled to adopt in them. 'Surely
it must be a strange Religion that must
be maintained by ungodly practices.
There never was any Religion that
allowed such practices.' [2] We must remember that CARLETON could remember
the Massacre of St. Bartholomew, the repeated attempts to assassinate ELIZABETH,
the successful assassinations by Popish
fanatics of WILLIAM THE SILENT and
HENRY IV., the Gunpowder Plot, and
the terrible history of the Netherlands.

[1] P. 89.   [2] P. 65.

It is no marvel that to his generation the Roman Church appeared to be identified with cynical wickedness. 'GOD will not have His Catholic Church maintained with lies, with wicked and ungracious practices, with treasons and rebellion, with conspiracies; they who practise such things can never prove themselves to be the Catholic Church: but the true Catholic Church is known by holding the Oracles of GOD, by worshipping GOD according to His own Oracles, by suffering patiently the practices of wicked men, by committing their cause to GOD, by trusting in GOD and in the power of His might, and by miraculous deliverances out of danger by the only hand and power of GOD. This holy and heavenly protection of GOD of the Church of England may plainly prove unto all the world, that the Church of England is a part and true member of that Catholic Church that serveth GOD in truth and sincerity, enjoying those privileges and favours which

GOD doth vouchsafe to no people saving
to His own Church.'[1]   He ends with
'some considerations proposed to such
as are not well affected to Religion.'
Among these we find the following:
'Withal they may be pleased to consider
the Works of GOD, His protection and
miraculous defence of His Church; which
miraculous defence hath appeared here
over the Church of England, as also elsewhere, but more conspicuous here: more
illustrious examples of GOD's mercy will
hardly be found anywhere; GOD hath
for many years delivered this Church,
preserved us in peace, when all the
Nations about us have been in bloody
wars.'[2]   Bishop CARLETON was representative of loyal Anglicans; at the Synod
of Dort, which he had attended at the
command of the King, he had distinguished himself by his protest against
the decree which seemed to disallow
episcopacy; yet his general attitude is

[1] P. 237.   [2] P. 290.

Puritan. The views which he expressed as unquestionably Anglican in 1624 had become characteristic of the anti-Laudian Puritans who were prepared to abolish Episcopacy itself twenty years later. That change is the salient feature of the period, and it wrecked the Establishment.

The Church of England, for which Bishop CARLETON so confidently claimed the signal and public approbation of the ALMIGHTY, was before all things a Protestant Church, standing in the van of the grand conflict with Antichrist as he was embodied in the apostate Church of Rome. This temper of mind and this point of view are notably exhibited in the 'Judgment concerning Toleration of Religion,' drawn up in 1626 by the Irish Bishops headed by Archbishop USSHER, the most learned churchman of the age. There it is stated that to tolerate the religion of `Papists would be a grievous sin implying a guilty condonation of 'the abominations of popery,' and, in the actual

circumstances which determined the proposition, nothing less than a shameful
'setting Religion for sale.' When such
were the views of scholars and bishops,
what were likely to be the opinions of
ardent and illiterate zealots? A rigidly
intolerant Protestant Church was, in the
temper of that age, the only kind of
Church which seemed fully entitled to
the privileges of a quasi-miraculous protection such as ancient Israel was recorded to have enjoyed. When CHARLES
and LAUD broke with this conception of
Anglicanism, and adopted a more reasonable attitude towards the older Church,
they seemed to many, and they the most
devout and patriotic of Englishmen, to be
endangering the prime condition of Divine
favour. Their political folly obscured and
prejudiced their religious policy in the
eyes of the nation, and has weighed
heavily against them in the verdict of
posterity. A spirit of suspicion was
aroused in the more ardent Puritans,

which sometimes passed into a settled
aversion. The Established Church succeeded to the abhorrence which had been
felt towards the Church of Rome, and lay
the more open to attack, since it was itself
a reformed Church, appealing against the
traditional system to the supreme authority
of the written Word. That written Word
was the arsenal of its adversaries. For
the Bible, when closely studied and
directly applied, offered to the devout
student another figure than that of the
Royal Vicegerent of JEHOVAH. In its
sacred record the Prophet stood out in
even more impressive prominence than
the King as the spokesman of the Divine
Mind, and the instrument of the Divine
Will. Both the King and the Prophet
were naturally set over against the Hierarchy, its critics, its rivals, sometimes its
victims, always its appointed correctors.
If the Anglican apologist built his case
for the Royal Supremacy and the ecclesiastical system of which the Royal

Supremacy was the cornerstone, on the precedents and principles of the Jewish monarchy, and was finally led by his argument into the fantastic dogmas of unlimited obedience, passive resistance, non-resistance, Monarchical Divine Right, &c.; so the more logical and independent of the Puritans, building their revolt against the ceremonies of the Established Church on the precedents provided by the Jewish prophets, were ultimately carried into the confusions of an irrational and unrestrained religious individualism.

The conflict with the Established Church was based throughout on the Bible. Against the legal assumption of Christian membership, which underlies the canons of 1604, and which was indeed implied in the Elizabethan Settlement, the separatists set the Biblical notion of a covenant freely and deliberately entered into by the Christian with his Maker. This Covenant exchanged between like-minded Christians was the basis of a sectarian or separatist Church. In 'the earliest completely developed Independent or Congregational Puritan (non-separatist) Catechism in existence'—I quote the description of Mr. CHAMPLIN BURRAGE—the question is proposed, 'How is a visible Church constituted and gathered?' The answer runs thus :—

'By a free mutual consent of Believers joining and covenanting to live as members of a holy Society together in all religious and virtuous duties as CHRIST and His Apostles did institute and practise in thé Gospel. By such a free mutual consent also all civil perfect Corporations did first begin.'

This answer naturally leads to the question how such an independent and covenanting congregation could be recon-

ciled with religious unity and civil order.
The answer is very important as illus-
trating a transitional phase of Puritan
thought when it had embraced the separatist principle, but still clung to the
national idea :—

> ' Unity in conscience standeth not
> upon one Church or Pastor over the
> rest, but upon the Word or Testa-
> ment of CHRIST taught ordinarily
> by that Church unto us whereof we
> are ; as GOD's Ordinance is.   Also
> thus most easily may the meanest
> next dwelling Magistrate rule any
> Church in outward peace ; yea in
> peace and concord of Religion far
> more easily and more readily than
> otherwise.'

Against the legally settled doctrines and
the officially commissioned Ministry the
sectary, basing himself always on his
personal study of the Bible, advanced

the revelations of truth made by the
Divine Spirit to the believer, and the
direct Divine inspirations vouchsafed to
Christian prophets.   A 'charismatic ministry' certified as genuine by its results
replaced in their minds the notion of a
ministry ordained to office by episcopal
or presbyteral ordination.

It is obvious that at every point the
sectary came into collision with the Established system.   JOHN PENRY says in his
Apology, written shortly before his death
in 1593, that the Scottish Presbyterians
objected against the Church of England
as doctrinally muzzled 'because they hear
that preachers are suspended, silenced,
imprisoned, and deprived,' and therefore
'think that little or no truth is permitted,
to be taught in England,' and that 'that
which is taught is measured by the length
of her Majesty's sceptre.'   The substantial
truth of this estimate of the ecclesiastical
situation in England cannot be disputed,
but the circumstances which reconciled

sensible Englishmen to such an anomalous state of things were neither trivial
nor irreligious. In point of fact the sectaries failed to make any considerable
impression on the English people, until
the political mismanagement of CHARLES I.
had created so much suspicion and exas-
peration, that the mere fact of antagonism
to the established Government was a
sufficient passport to popular favour.

So long as the Established Church
served visibly the interest of Protestant
Religion, even those who were strongly
Puritan regarded with disfavour all sugges-
tions of open separation from the national
worship. The violence and fanaticism
of the sectaries shocked sober-minded
Christians. Sober-minded Puritans could
not be hustled by the impetuous logic of
illiterate enthusiasts into a wholesale condemnation of a Church which had num-
bered among its founders and teachers
the most widely venerated of Protestant
divines, which had been illustrated by

the martyrs, and which counted among
its ministers the most earnest preachers
in the country. Moreover, Puritanism
was strongly entrenched among the
country gentlemen and the commercial
class, neither of whom were likely to
approve the constant religious bickerings
and the wild licence of opinion which
marked the sectarian congregations in
Holland, which had become the refuge
of religious outcasts of every kind. Not
until the ecclesiastical policy of Archbishop LAUD had alarmed and alienated
the Puritan laity did Englishmen begin
to look more complacently on those who
set themselves against the familiar and
valued ideal of religious establishment.
The outbreak of the Civil War gave a
terrible shock to the whole fabric of
society, and stimulated every element of
discontent and disorder. There was a
sudden and alarming outbreak of sectarianism. The army of the Parliament
became a school of religious anarchy.

The most eminent Puritan of the time, RICHARD BAXTER, has left on record his amazement and horror, when he suddenly found himself in contact with this new phenomenon. After the victory of Naseby he had visited the army of CROMWELL, to learn the fate of some friends who had been engaged in the battle :—

    ' When I found them, I stayed with them a night, and I understood the state of the Army much better than ever I had done before. We that lived quietly in Coventry did keep to our old principles, and thought all others had done so too, except a very few inconsiderable persons. . . . We took the true happiness of King and People, Church and State, to be our end, and so we understood the Covenant, engaging both against Papists and Schismaticks ; and when the Court News-book told the world

of the swarms of Anabaptists in our
armies, we thought it had been a
mere lie, because it was not so with
us, nor in any of the garrisons or
county forces about us. But when
I came to the Army among CROM-
WELL'S soldiers I found a new face
of things which I never dreamed
of : I heard the plotting heads very
hot upon that which intimated their
intention to subvert both Church
and State. Independency and Ana-
baptistery were most prevalent ;
Antinomianism and Arminianism
were equally distributed.'

BAXTER observed the dangerous ming-
ling of political with religious theories,
and the driving force of a fanaticism
which respected no limits beyond its
own will, and no guidance apart from
its own visions.

'They said, What were the Lords
of England but WILLIAM THE CON-

QUEROR's Colonels? or the Barons
but his Majors? or the Knights but
his Captains? They plainly shewed
me that they thought GOD's Providence would cast the trust of Religion
and the Kingdom upon them as
conquerors : they made nothing of
all the most wise and godly in the
Armies and Garrisons, that were not
of their way. *Per fas aut nefas*, by
law or without it, they were resolved to take down, not only
Bishops and Liturgy and Ceremonies,
but all that did withstand their
way. They were far from thinking
of a moderate Episcopacy, or of any
healing way between the Episcopal
and the Presbyterians : they most
honoured the Separatists, Anabaptists, and Antinomians : but
CROMWELL and his Council took on
them to join themselves to no party,
but to be for the liberty of all.'

Rather against CROMWELL'S wishes
BAXTER set himself to argue the soldiers
out of their extravagant opinions. He
found that under all their absurdities they
had got hold of one great idea, which
they were not indeed themselves competent to understand or apply in practice,
and which the eager and noble-minded
Puritan was quite unable to appreciate,
but which in the retrospect of a later
age is seen to have been sound and
fruitful :—

' I found that many honest men of
weak judgments and little acquaint-
ance with such matters, had been
seduced into a disputing vein, and
made it too much of their religion
to talk for this opinion and for
that : sometimes for State Democracy, and sometimes for Church
Democracy ; sometimes against forms
of prayer, and sometimes against
infant baptism (which yet some of

them did maintain); sometimes
against set times of prayer, and
against the tying of ourselves to
any duty before the Spirit move us,
and sometimes about Free Grace and
Free Will, and all the points of
Antinomianism and Arminianism.
So that I was almost always, when
I had opportunity, disputing with
one or other of them: sometimes
for our civil government, and sometimes for Church order and government: sometimes for infant baptism,
and oft against Antinomianism and
the contrary extreme. But their
most frequent and vehement disputes
were for LIBERTY OF CONSCIENCE, as
they called it; that is, that the Civil
Magistrate had nothing to do to determine of anything in Matters of
Religion, by constraint or restraint,
but every man might not only hold,
but preach and do in matters of
religion what he pleased; that the

Civil Magistrate hath nothing to do but with civil things, to keep the peace, and protect the Church's liberties, &c.'[1]

RICHARD BAXTER's feeling with respect to the military sectaries was thoroughly representative of the Puritans. It were unjust to deny that it had large justification. For the bold advocates of ' Liberty of Conscience' were far indeed from any adequate understanding of their own case. Their arguments were strangely illustrated by the wrecking of churches, accompanied too often by shocking profanities. Indeed, they were destined to provoke such resentment by their doctrinal extravagances and the violence of their political methods, as to throw back for a whole generation the cause of religious Toleration. For there are two factors requisite in a successful advocacy of such ' Liberty of Con-

[1] v. Life, ed. Sylvester, pp. 50, 53, A.D. 1696.

science' as the sectaries clamoured for. There must not only be a strong sense of the rights of one's own conscience, but a genuine respect for the consciences of others. The one factor the Sectaries possessed in full measure. There never was a generation so obsessed with conscientious scruples, so quixotically loyal to its perceptions of religious truth, so insistent on the exact harmonising of theory and practice. But the other factor was almost universally absent. The sectaries paid no regard whatever to the conscientious beliefs of the Papist, the Anglican, and the Presbyterian. They saw no incongruity between claiming 'liberty of conscience,' and imposing their own arbitrary notions of social morality by main force on a reluctant majority, or wounding the deepest sentiments of reverence by their rough handling of the churches. Even the Quakers, who embodied a protest, not against the Church of CHARLES and LAUD, but against the system which had been improvised to replace it, sullied their reputation for genuine tolerance by extravagances which were justly offensive to pious consciences, and go far to explain, and in some sense to excuse, the severities with which they were treated. In the seventeenth century all parties were intolerant, and something must be allowed to those who first inscribed on their political banner the noble ideal 'Liberty of Conscience'; but we may not forget their incompetence for the championship of that cause, or refuse to allow to their opponents and persecutors such apologies as their undoubted extravagance provided.

It is worth noting that the Sects, though they caused widespread consternation, and in the Civil War obtained a brief tenure of power, did not commend themselves to any large proportion of the English people. A very careful writer estimates that 'at no time before 1630, and possibly even before 1640, can there have been

more than five or six hundred genuine
Brownists or Barrowists in England, while
the presence of even a smaller number
would exceed reasonable probability.'[1]
'In 1626,' we are told, 'the total number
of Anabaptists in the five congregations in
England was at least one hundred and
fifty.'[2] 'Before 1645 neither Separatism
nor Independent Puritanism seems to
have been really strong in London.
Says ROBERT BAILLIE in 1645 : 'For the
Brownists, their number at London or
Amsterdam is but very small.' The Independent Puritans of London he likewise
reports 'as yet to consist of much within
one thousand persons ; men, women, and
all who to this day have put themselves in
any known congregation of that way,
being reckoned. But setting aside number, for other respects they are of so
eminent a condition, that not any nor all

[1] v. Champlin Burrage, 'The Early English Dissenters,' vol. i. p. 152.
[2] v. Ibid., p. 273.

the rest of the Sects are comparable to them.' [1]

Modern Dissent may be traced to the sectaries of the Commonwealth so far as the theories of its organisation and its attitude towards the Established Church are concerned, but its strong hold on the middle classes of this country, and its avoidance of the extravagant features of its denominational progenitors, are derived from the Puritans who by a calamitous blunder were extruded from the National System at the Restoration.

[1] v. Ibid., p. 311.

PURITANISM AS A WORKING SYSTEM

V

PURITANISM AS A WORKING SYSTEM

RICHARD BAXTER is the Saint of Puritanism, and he is also its most illustrious exponent. Born in 1615, when the first JAMES was reigning, he lived until 1691, three years after the second JAMES had been driven from the throne. Every phase of Puritanism is represented in his career. As a youth he was drawn to Nonconformity by its association with a purer morality than was commonly insisted upon in the Established Church. He had, however, no scruples with respect to the doctrine and government of the Church from which he received Baptism, Confirmation, and Ordination, until the severities to the Puritans offended his conscience, and the Laudian movement alarmed his reason. During the Commonwealth he was a Protagonist in the war with the Sects, and foremost among the advocates of reconciliation with the Episcopalians. Taking no mean part in the Restoration, he seemed marked out for a commanding position in the re-established National Church. But he divined too clearly the direction in which the restored Anglicans were moving, and refused the Bishoprick of Hereford when it was offered to him. He shared to the full the calamities which befell the defeated Puritans, and finally ended his days as a tolerated Dissenter.

BAXTER is the typical Puritan pastor at his best. In both the characteristic methods of Puritan pastorate—preaching and religious writing—he was supreme. When his frequent illnesses hindered him from preaching, he betook himself to writing evangelistic and devotional tracts and treatises, which enjoyed an immense circulation in his life-time, and have survived in some cases until the present time in the use of religious people. Finally, when he was silenced by the Authorities of Church and State, he continued to pour out a stream of edifying compositions, which extended and deepened the remarkable spiritual influence which he had acquired. His latest published tractate is stated on the title-page to have been ' recommended to the Bookseller a few days before his death, to be immediately printed for the good of souls,' and is designed as an answer to the Philippian gaoler's question, ' *Sirs, what must I do to be saved?*' BAXTER'S whole life was, indeed, filled with the attempt to answer first for himself, and then for others, that all-important question.

Any just review of Puritanism must include an appreciation of the influence of the popular religious literature which it inspired. Sir JAMES STEPHEN, in his well-known Essay, commented on the striking weakness of the Established Church in this respect. 'Rich beyond all Protestant rivalry in sacred literature,' he says, 'the Church of England, from the days of PARKER to those of LAUD, had scarcely produced any one considerable work of popular instruction.' His reflections on this fact are as suggestive as they are severe :—

'There is no parallel in the annals of any other Protestant State of so wonderful a concentration, and so imperfect a diffusion of learning and genius, of piety and zeal. The reigns of WHITGIFT, BANCROFT, and LAUD were unmolested by cares so rude as those of evangelising the artisans and peasantry. JEWEL and BULL, HALL and DONNE, HOOKER and TAYLOR, lived and wrote for their peers and for future ages, but not for the commonalty of their own. Yet was not Christianity bereft in England of her distinctive and glorious privilege? It was still the religion of the poor. Amidst persecution, contempt, and penury, the Puritans had toiled and suffered and had not rarely died in their 'service.'

Dr. GROSART quotes and comments on these words. 'I know not,' he says, 'that a more damning charge could be brought against a Church.'[1] It is, however, to be pointed out, that the earlier Puritans were almost without exception beneficed clergymen of the Church of England; that the Bishops, in exerting themselves to reform and establish the system of parochial and diocesan administration, were doing an indispensable work of the highest importance; and, finally, that the learned defence of

[1] v. 'Representative Nonconformists,' by Rev. A. B. Grosart (Hodder & Stoughton, 1879).

Protestantism, which the Anglican champions provided, served as a wall behind which the Puritans could carry on in safety their excellent work of popularising religion in England. It is not necessary to belittle the achievement of the Anglican, in order to do justice to that of the Puritan. The nature and importance of the latter are, however, too little recognised by modern Churchmen, and for this reason it is requisite to emphasise both.

The Jesuits had early perceived the weakness of Protestantism on its devotional side, and had set themselves to the task of providing at a very cheap rate popularly written tractates which would appeal to the emotions, especially of the young. There can be no doubt that their efforts were rewarded with a large measure of success. Among the undergraduates at the Universities a perceptible impression was made, and there were many converts to Romanism. In 1595

the Vice-Chancellor and Heads of Cambridge had complained to Archbishop
WHITGIFT that 'things had grown to
that pass that there were no books
more ordinarily bought than Popish
writers.'[1]   Now an antidote was provided.   The devotional writings of the
Jesuits, inspired by the ascetic spirit
of the Medieval Church, raised to heroic
exaltation by the passions and risks of
the great conflict with Protestantism,
were met by another kind of religious
composition, not less moving and far
more virile, which drew its inspiration,
not from the failing wells of asceticism,
but from the perpetual springs of the
Gospel.   The two types of literature
were curiously combined in BAXTER'S
memory of the process of his own
conversion.   Like the youthful AUGUSTINE,
his boyish conscience was stirred into
activity by remorse for robbing an
orchard :—

[1] v. Strype's, 'Life of Whitgift,' book iv. chap. xiv.

'And being under some more conviction for my sin, a poor Day-
labourer in the Town . . . had an old
torn book which he lent my father,
which was called " Bunny's Resolu-
tion," being written by PARSONS the
Jesuit, and corrected by EDMUND
BUNNY. . . . And in the reading of
this book, when I was about fifteen
years of age, it pleased GOD to
awaken my soul, and shew me the
folly of sinning, and the misery of
the wicked, and the unexpressible
weight of things eternal, and the
necessity of resolving on a holy
life, more than I was ever acquainted
with before.'[1]

Subsequently he got hold of other and
better devotional books :—

'It pleased GOD that a poor pedlar
came to the door that had ballards

[1] v. Life. p. 3.

and some good books. And my father bought of him Dr. Sibb's "Bruized Reed." This also I read, and found it suited to my state, and seasonably sent me ; which opened more the Love of God to me, and gave me a livelier apprehension of the mystery of Redemption, and how much I was beholden to Jesus Christ.'

In this statement we get a glimpse of the manner of circulating this new literature of religion. Pedlars offered them along with the ballards which at that time were so popular and so influential. Baxter proceeds in his autobiography :—

'After this we had a servant that had a little piece of Mr. Perkins's Works, of "Repentance" and the "Right Art of Living and Dying Well," and the "Government of the

Tongue." And the reading of that did further inform me and confirm me. And thus, without any means but books was GOD pleased to resolve me for Himself.'

Thus, from the very start of his religious life, BAXTER had reason to think highly of books as instruments of evangelising the people ; and of all the Puritans he did most in providing the kind of books required. One of his works, 'The Saint's Everlasting Rest,' has taken its place as a devotional classic. As a parish minister he attached importance to instructing the people by means of short and clearly expressed Catechisms.

The defeat of the King drew with it the collapse of the ecclesiastical system. For twenty years, from 1640 to 1660, the National Church was in the melting-pot of experiment and revolution. It is not quite easy to understand what actually happened.

Perhaps a third of the benefices were sequestrated, the incumbents being evicted on various charges, some for being Royalists, some for being Laudians, some for being incompetent, some for being morally scandalous. The clergy were unpopular and defenceless, and there can be no reasonable doubt that they were treated with great harshness. The Prayer-book was prohibited, and Episcopacy, together with the whole disciplinary system administered by the Bishops, was abolished, but the Directory drawn up by the Westminster Assembly, and imposed by Parliament on the country, was hardly anywhere put in use, and the Presbyterian system was so alien to English modes of thinking and living, that it was never seriously enforced outside London, and some parts of Lancashire. Thus there was a strangely anomalous situation created. The 'Triers,' who were really an Ecclesiastical Commission clothed with Parliamentary authority, and charged with making spiritual provision for the parishes, appear on the whole to have acted conscientiously ; and by slow degrees a working system was improvised, which drew into the religious service of the nation the best men of all descriptions who would undertake to accept the existing Government. There was much confusion, and a great outbreak of sectarian fanaticism ; and these in the retrospect obscured every other aspect of the time, so that it became in common speech the synonym of a reign of licentious hypocrisy. But the more closely the period of the Commonwealth is studied, the more untrue this version of it is seen to be. Along with the confusion and fanaticism proceeded a solid religious work, a process of strong moral education, which sobered and raised the national character, and left its mark for good on the national religion. Puritanism for the first and last time was dominant, and could give unimpeded expression to its principles. Both its strength and its weakness came into prominence.

BAXTER's famous ministry at Kidderminster
illustrates the theory of pastorate which
had been expressed in numerous Puritan
works, and nowhere more admirably than
in his own 'Reformed Pastor,' a composition which ranks next to the 'Saint's Everlasting Rest' in popularity, and, hardly less
than that composition, deserves the title,
classical.   No student of Puritanism ought
to omit a study of both these works, or
leave unread BAXTER's remarkable Autobiography.

The legal instrument appointing BAXTER
preacher at Kidderminster is dated April
5, 1641, and is signed by about thirty
persons.   He thus describes the circumstances in which it was sent :—

'The town of Kederminster, in
Worcestershire, drew up a Petition
against their Ministers : the Vicar
of the place they articled against
as one that was utterly insufficient
for the ministry, presented by a

papist, unlearned, preached but once a quarter, which was so weakly as exposed him to laughter, and persuaded them that he understood not the very substantial articles of Christianity ; that he frequented Alehouses, and had sometimes been drunk ; that he turned the Table Altar-wise, &c., with more such as this. . . . The people put their petition into the hands of Sir Henry Herbert, Burgess for Bewdley, a town two miles distant. The Vicar knowing his insufficiency . . . desired to compound the business with them ; and by the mediation of Sir Henry Herbert and others, it was brought to this, That he should, instead of his present curate in the town, allow £60 per annum to a Preacher whom fourteen of them nominated should choose; and that he should not hinder this Preacher from preaching whenever he pleased, and that he himself should

read Common-prayer, and do all else
that was to be done ; and so they
preferred not their petition against
him, nor against his curates ; but he
kept his place, which was worth to
him near £200 per Annum, allowing
that £60 out of it to their Lecturer.
. . . Hereupon they invited me to
them from Bridgnorth ; the Bailiff of
the town, and all the Feoffees, desired
me to preach with them, in order to
a full determination. My mind was
much to the place as soon as it was
described to me ; because it was a
full congregation and most convenient
temple ; an ignorant, rude, and re-
velling people for the greater part,
who had need of preaching ; and yet
had among them a small company of
converts, who were humble, godly,
and of good conversations, and not
much hated by the rest, and therefore
the fitter to assist their Teacher ; but
above all because they had hardly

ever had any lively serious preaching among them. . . . As soon as I came to Kiderminster, and had preached there one day, I was chosen *Nemine contradicente* (for though fourteen only had the power of choosing, they desired to please the rest). And thus I was brought by the gracious Providence of GOD to that place which had the chiefest of my labours, and yielded me the greatest fruits of comfort.' [1]

The ministry thus happily begun was interrupted by the Civil War, for BAXTER had thrown in his lot with the Parliament, and even (as he subsequently regretted) had subscribed the Solemn League and Covenant, while Worcestershire generally had taken sides with the King. Accordingly, for some years he was engaged, partly in combating the sectarianism of CROMWELL's army, and partly in writing

[1] Life, p. 19, 20.

books. When at length peace was restored by the total ruin of the Royal
cause, the people of Kidderminster re-
sumed their opposition to the Vicar and
his Curates, and succeeded in obtaining
the sequestration of the living. Then they
offered the vacant benefice to BAXTER,
who would only consent to take again the
Lectureship which he had formerly held.
He returned to Kidderminster in a regu-
larly covenanted relation to the people :—

' I went to Kidderminster . . . and
the people again vehemently urged me
to take the Vicarage : which I denied,
and got the magistrates and burgesses
together into the Town Hall, and told
them that (though I was offered many
hundred pounds per annum elsewhere)
I was willing to continue with them
in my old Lecturer's place which I had
before the wars, expecting they should
make the maintenance an hundred
pounds a year, and a house : and if

they would promise to submit to that doctrine of Christ which, as his Minister, I should deliver to them, proved by the Holy Scriptures, I would not leave them. . . . This Covenant was drawn up between us in Articles, and subscribed, in which I disclaimed the Vicarage and pastoral charge of the parish, and only undertook the Lecture.' [1]

The Ministry thus conditioned was carried on for about fourteen years, in spite of repeated interruptions by illness. It will be worth while to have before us BAXTER's own account of his pastoral work : it will appear that he was far indeed from being merely a preacher :—

'I preached before the wars twice each LORD'S Day : but after the war but once, and once every Thursday, besides occasional sermons. Every Thursday evening

[1] v. Life, p. 79.

my neighbours that were most desirous and had opportunity, met at my house, and there one of them repeated the Sermon, and afterwards they proposed what doubts any of them had about the sermon, or any other case of conscience, and I resolved their doubts : and last of all I caused sometimes one, and sometimes another of them to pray, to exercise them ; and sometimes I prayed with them myself : which, besides singing a psalm, was all they did. And once a week also some of the younger sort who were not fit to pray in so great an assembly, met among a few more privately, where they spent three hours in praying together : every Saturday night they met at some of their houses to repeat the sermon of the last LORD's Day, and to pray and prepare themselves for the following day. Once in a few weeks we had a day of humiliation

on one occasion or another. Every
religious woman that was safely
delivered, instead of the old feast-
ings and gossipings, if they were
able, did keep a day of thanksgiving
with some of their neighbours with
them, praising GOD and singing
psalms, and soberly feasting together.
Two days every week my assistant
and myself took fourteen families
between us for private catechising
and conference, he going through
the parish, and the town coming to
me. I first heard them recite the
words of the Catechism, and then
examined them about the sense, and
lastly urged them with all possible
engaging reason and vehemency to
answerable affection and practice.
. . . I spent about an hour with
a family, and admitted no others to
be present, lest bashfulness should
make it burdensome, or any should
talk of the weaknesses of others : so

that all the afternoons on Mondays
and Tuesdays I spent in this after
I had begun it, for it was many
years before I did attempt it : and
my Assistant spent the mornings of
the same days in the same employment. Before that I only catechised
them in the Church ; and conferred
with, now and then, one occasionally.

' Besides all this, I was forced for
five or six years by the people's
necessity to practise physick : a
common pleurisy happening one
year, and no physician being near,
I was forced to advise them, to save
their lives : and I could not afterwards avoid the importunity of the
town and country round about : and
because I never once took a penny
of any one, I was crowded with
patients, so that almost twenty would
be at my door at once : and though
GOD, by more success than I
expected, so long encouraged me,

yet at last I could endure it no
longer, partly because it hindered
my other studies, and partly because
the very fear of miscarrying and
doing any one harm, did make it
an intolerable burden to me. So
that after some years' practice, I
procured a godly diligent physician
to come and live in the town, and
bound myself by promise to practise
no more, unless in consultation with
him in case of any seeming necessity ;
and so with that answer I turned
them all off, and never meddled with
it more. But all these my labours
(except my private conferences with
the families) even preaching and
preparing for it, were but my
recreations, and as it were the work
of my spare hours. For my writings
were my chiefest daily labour, which
yet went the more slowly on, that
I never one hour had an Amanuensis
to dictate to, and specially because

my weakness took up so much of my time. . . .

'Besides all these, every first Wednesday of the month was our monthly meeting for parish discipline; and every first Thursday of the month was the Ministers' meeting for discipline and disputation: and in those disputations it fell to my lot to be almost constant Moderator; and for every such day, usually, I prepared a written determination. All which I mention as my mercies and delights, and not as my burdens. And every Thursday besides, I had the company of divers Godly ministers at my house after the Lecture, with whom I spent that afternoon in the truest recreation, till my neighbours came to meet for their exercise of repetition and prayer. For ever blessed be the God of mercies that brought me from the grave, and gave me after

wars and sickness, fourteen years'
liberty in such sweet employment.' [1]

Such a ministry was a revelation
of Christian pastorate, and enriched
English religion with an ideal of pastoral
duty which has never since been wholly
lost.   It was truly a noble and gracious
thing, one of the *magnalia Dei* for
which the Church blesses GOD.   As a
human achievement it is unparalleled, for
it must be remembered that the man who
was carrying on this varied and laborious
ministry, was at the same time the foremost controversialist in England, and
closely concerned in the general politicks
of the time.   We know not which to
wonder at most, the versatility of his
genius, or the militant force of his faith.
BAXTER'S pastoral solicitude is Pauline.
'Our greatest afflictions,' he said in his
farewell sermon on August 17, 1662,
'next to the misery of the ungodly, is to

[1] v. Life, pp. 83, 84.

think of our weak ones, what will become of them.' This, indeed, was the principal root of his polemical ardour. No doubt the natural eagerness of his temperament, and a fondness for the intellectual exercise of disputation contributed, but the main consideration was certainly pastoral. He felt himself set to watch over his people, and defend them from attack. The sectary was in his eyes primarily one who was endangering the spiritual safety of the '*babes in Christ*.' His charity was apostolic, and inspired his constant pursuit of ecclesiastical unity. If his opponents might fairly say of his peace-making labour what NEWMAN said of PUSEY's 'Eirenicon,' that it was 'an olive-branch discharged from a catapult,' the explanation lies, not in any failure of sincerity, but in a curious lack of tactical wisdom which marked his public course, and is the more surprising since in his personal ministries his zeal was softened and sweetened by a winning sympathy.

Sectarianism was repulsive to his large-
ness of heart, as well as disgusting to his
reason.   Hence his horror of separation,
and his passionate zeal for unity.   Even
when his cause had been defeated, and he
himself was about to be silenced, he could
not bring himself to say anything which
could   seem   to   suggest   or   justify
separatism.   His   farewell   sermon   in-
cludes an earnest warning against schismatic tendencies :—

    ' Be sure you understand the nature
of Church union, and necessity of
maintaining it, and abhor all ways
that are truly schismatical, that would
rend and divide the Church of
CHRIST.   As you must not, under
pretence of avoiding Schism, cast
your soul upon apparent hazard of
damnation, so you must maintain
the necessity of Church-union and
communion : when CHRIST'S members
walk in communion with CHRIST'S

members, supposing that which is
singular to the generality of judicious
men, take heed of anything that
would withdraw you from the communion of the generality of those
that are sound in the faith. Take
heed of withdrawing from the main
body of believers. CHRIST is the
Head of His Church; He will never
condemn His Church : walk in those
substantials CHRIST's Church hath
walked in.   Division amongst Christians is a sin GOD hath described
as odious and tending to the ruin
of Christians. Be very suspicious
of any that would draw you from
the main body of believers, and
keep communion with the universal
Church of CHRIST, with the generality of the godly in love and
affection.'

When from the devoted and indefatig-
able Pastor, 'whose praise is in all the

churches,' we pass to a consideration of his methods, we are brought into no slight perplexity. Can it be maintained that the Puritan system, so admirably illustrated at Kidderminster, was suitable for general adoption? Its effectiveness at the time was undoubtedly very great. BAXTER could point to remarkable results as following from his ministry; but was his system capable of general application? Did it not depend too much on the zeal, wisdom, and ability of the pastor himself? BAXTER was no ordinary man; yet we may safely say that BAXTER alone could have made this system tolerable for any length of time. In the hands of the average minister it would quickly sink into an insufferable infliction, or a lifeless form. ' BAXTER'S contribution to the history of the Pastoral Ideal was not the successful introduction of the parochial method, which he so earnestly practised and so passionately advocated : but the example

he gave to his own generation, and
left on record to posterity, of the pastoral
life.   He stood midway between the two
great contending views of Church organisation.   His evangelistic ardour drew
him to the parochial system, which,
with whatever faults, assumed that the
clergyman had a direct mission to the
whole population of the parish.   He
could not acquiesce in a view which,
however otherwise reasonable, left the
bulk of the people outside the activities
of the clergy.   On the other hand, his
austere ideal of Christian holiness, his
righteous loathing of the hypocrisies of
the Established system, his intense conviction that morality was the very mark
of a Church . . . all led him to look with
kindness on that notion of "gathered
Churches" which was common both to
the Independents and the Anabaptists.
He endeavoured to combine the opposed
views in his system at Kidderminster.
He applied the close personal discipline

of a congregation to a parish. Great as
his success was, it fell so far short of
what he needed to justify his position,
that his attempt must be described as
a splendid failure. Of the 1,400 Church
members in Kidderminster, only 600
accepted his government; for the rest
he had no effectual system. He would
not coerce to Communion as the Bishops
had done : he would suppress by the
magistrate's authority the open violation
of the Moral law, which the Bishops
had professed to desire, but had never
seriously attempted. When the State
was hostile, even this necessary measure
of coercion failed to be possible. He
was surely drifting into the position
of the sectaries whom he loathed. Perhaps the conflict between parochialism
with its territorial basis of ecclesiastical
rights, and Christianity, with its personal
basis, is not capable of satisfactory
appeasement. It must be recognised
that the parish priest of an Established

Church combines in his person two sets of duties. He is a pastor, and he is a State official: he is the minister of CHRIST, and the servant of the nation. BAXTER could never thus divide his personality: he was altogether and exclusively a consecrated person. Hence the unreconciled contradictions of his conception of pastoral duty.'[1]

Apart from the questions of ecclesiastical system and pastoral method, can it be denied that the Puritan conception of Christianity, so nobly expressed in the ministry of RICHARD BAXTER, was itself too narrow and personal for ultimate acceptance by a National Church? When one attempts to realise the type of citizen which would be fashioned by that conception, one must needs feel that in certain particulars of great importance it would have been seriously defective. BAXTER'S intense conviction that the sole end of a rightly ordered

[1] v. 'Cross-bench Views,' p. 172.

human life is to prepare for Death; his continually recurring note of sombre urgency which gives distinctive colour to his religious writings: his ascetical contempt of everything which came into competition with this absorbing consideration: his exalted 'other-worldliness,' to use a convenient if often abused expression—all are difficult to reconcile with the claims, interests, and ramifying relations of national life Puritanism addressed itself to some elements only of human nature, the noblest elements assuredly, but still not on that account competent to claim exclusive attention. It produced, therefore, a strong, exalted, magnanimous type of citizen, but one that was limited, hard, and liable to dangerous and sudden failure. Its danger lay in its very exaltation. The æsthetic, social, and intellectual faculties were starved by this undue concentration on the spiritual and the ethical. Human nature takes its revenge on every violation done, with whatever excuses, to its integrity : and Puritanism drew down upon itself no less a calamity than that which is implied in such a catastrophe. We must conclude, therefore, that the explanations both of its brief success, and of its final failure, must be sought partly in the extraordinary conditions of the age which witnessed both, but mainly in its own defects as a version of Christianity claiming national recognition and enforcement.

THE RESTORATION SETTLE-
MENT

VI

THE RESTORATION SETTLEMENT

WHEN the Monarchy was restored in 1660, a new ecclesiastical settlement was generally regarded as inevitable. The existing system or quasi-system was clearly provisional. It had no secure basis in law, and it expressed no widely-distributed popular demand. That Episcopacy must in some form be restored was indeed everywhere assumed. The Monarchy and the Episcopal Church had been so intimately connected since the Reformation, had stood together so closely through the long conflict, had suffered and fallen together in the wars, and had together shared the bitter consequence of defeat, that the restoration of the one was seen to involve that of the other. But it was not less clearly perceived that the ecclesiastical system could not rightly be restored without alteration. The causes of the Rebellion had been as much religious as civil, and the Restoration would not be secure, if it failed to commend itself to the religious opinion of the country. Moreover, the actual circumstances in which the Restoration was effected seemed to necessitate such a revision of the ecclesiastical system as would satisfy the general body of Puritans, who were now commonly called Presbyterians. These had taken an important part in bringing back the King. For some while before the Restoration private negotiations had been proceeding between the leading ministers in England and the more moderate of the Royalist divines, and there can be no doubt that language had been freely used which was fairly understood as promising a genuinely moderate and reconciling policy. Care was taken to emphasise the attachment of CHARLES to the Protestant religion. ' I am very glad the King was at the Protestant churches,' wrote Bishop MORLEY from Breda to COSIN in February, 1660, when the prospect of a restoration seemed to lie wholly in the goodwill of the Presbyterians and moderate Anglicans, ' which gives great satisfaction to those ministers here to whom I have told it. I wish there were not some of our clergy too rigid in that particular.' [1] The Declaration from Breda (April 4–14, 1660) was studiously vague, but its expressions could not in the circumstances be read otherwise than as a promise of large concessions to those who were actually in possession of the parishes at the time :—

  ' And because the passion and un-charitableness of the times have pro-

[1] v. Cosin's Correspondence, part i. p. 291. Surtees Society.

duced several opinions in religion, by which men are engaged in parties and animosities against each other; (which, when they shall hereafter unite in a freedom of conversation, will be composed, or better understood), we do declare a liberty to tender consciences, and that no man shall be disquieted, or called in question, for differences of opinion in matters of religion, which do not disturb the peace of the kingdom; and that we shall be ready to consent to such an Act of Parliament, as, upon mature deliberation, shall be offered to us, for the full granting that indulgence.'

In this specious reference to Parliament lay the promise of the great betrayal which was soon to be disclosed. For, once arrived in England, CHARLES found himself far stronger than he had supposed. Many elements entered into the outburst of enthusiasm with which the restored exile was welcomed. The Puritan domination had borne hardly on great sections of the community. The capricious military despotism, into which statesmanship had degenerated, had thrown into revolt the self-respect of ordinary Englishmen, and the old constitutional system, of which the King was the symbol, appealed to them with irresistible force. This astonishing explosion of long-suppressed monarchical sentiment swept away all moderating considerations, and seemed to cancel all obligations. As a matter of course the Bishops and Clergy took again their legal position, and began to treat the existing incumbents as intruders. No less than 450 evictions appear to have taken place in the interval between the Restoration and the passing of the Act of Uniformity. The old Incumbents, who had either fled, or been driven away, during the interregnum, appeared, claimed their rights, and were admitted again to their former benefices,

the existing holders being summarily
thrust out without any consideration.
The Puritans found the situation changed
with dramatic suddenness to their disadvantage. They were no longer in a
position to dictate terms, or even to nego-
tiate ; they had the law against them in
the parishes, and cavalier feeling against
them in the nation. The sentiment of
Parliament, notably of the House of
Commons, was extremely hostile. They
had no backing of popular affection, and
for the moment little apparent hold on the
public conscience. Their only hope of
tolerable treatment lay in the King himself, and CHARLES could not, even if he
had wished, stand up against the flood-
tide of avenging Royalism which was
carrying all before it. Moreover, the
resolute intolerance of the Puritans themselves offered a hindrance to any effective
action on the King's part. For CHARLES
did undoubtedly dislike the policy which
he found himself compelled to sanction.

His policy was directed towards such a toleration of religious Dissenters as would enable him to show kindness to the Roman Catholics, to whom on many accounts, both personal and public, he was strongly attached. 'Rebel for rebel,' he scribbled to CLARENDON at a Council meeting, 'I had rather trust a Papist rebel than a Presbyterian.' When, however, at the Conference at Worcester House on October 22, 1660, CLARENDON proposed that liberty of worship should be granted to all law-abiding sectaries, the proposition was received by the Puritans with suggestive silence, until BAXTER gave expression to their feelings by insisting that some distinction must be made between 'parties tolerable and parties intolerable,' and that they could not consent to any Toleration of 'Papists and Socinians.' Thus the King, their only possible protector, was alienated by their conscientious but inexorable attitude of intolerance. The full disclosure of their helplessness was not made immediately. On October 25th, the King issued a Declaration, the terms of which had been previously submitted to the Puritan leaders, and which, if it had been made the basis of legislation, might have secured religious harmony. This document outlined a revision of the Episcopal system which would have reconciled most moderate Puritans to Episcopacy. Eight specific pledges were given, and general assurances of indulgence to scrupulous consciences were added. The pledges are the following :—

I. 'To take care that the Lord's Day be applied to holy exercises, without unnecessary divertisements,' and to insist upon good character in the case of all ministers appointed to office in the Church.

II. To 'appoint such a number of suffragan bishops in every diocese as shall be sufficient for the due performance of their work.'

III. To provide that 'no bishop shal ordain, or exercise any part of jurisdiction which appertains to the censures of the church, without the advice and assistance of the Presbyters,' and that lay-officials shall not 'exercise any act of spiritual jurisdiction.'

IV. To constitute the deans and chapters, together with an equal number of elected presbyters, a council for the bishops, who were not to exercise any part of their jurisdiction apart from them.

V. To 'take care that confirmation be rightly and solemnly performed, by the information, and with the consent of the minister of the place, who shall admit none to the Lord's Supper, till they have made a credible profession of their faith, and promised obedience to the Will of God,' and to take effectual steps to bar from Communion all unfit persons. It is provided that 'the rural dean and his assistants are in their respective divisions to see, that the children and younger sort be carefully instructed by the respective ministers of every parish, in the grounds of Christian religion, and be able to give a good account of their faith and knowledge, and also of their Christian conversation conformable thereunto, before they be confirmed by the bishop, or admitted to the sacrament of the Lord's Supper.'

VI. To provide that 'no bishop shall exercise any arbitrary power, or do or impose anything upon the clergy or the people, but what is according to the known law of the land.'

VII. To revise the Prayer Book, and add additional forms.

VIII. To leave the settlement of all disputed questions as to ceremonies 'to the advice of a national synod,' to be 'duly called after a little time, and a mutual conversation between persons of different persuasions hath mollified those distempers, abated those sharpnesses, and extinguished those jealousies, which make

men unfit for those consultations,' and to
secure that 'none shall be denied the
sacrament of the Lord's Supper, though
they do not use the gesture of kneeling
in the act of receiving.'

The use of the Cross in Baptism, bowing
at the Name of JESUS, the use of the
surplice, and the oath of canonical obedience, were 'in the meantime' to be op-
tional, and the mitigated subscription of
the Articles authorised by the statute of
the thirteenth of Queen Elizabeth was to
suffice for the tenure of benefices.

The King renews the promises made in
the Declaration from Breda, and declares
that the disturbances which have happened
since his arrival have had no authority in
any direction of his. 'Let us all endeavour,' concludes the document, 'and emu-
late each other in those endeavours, to
countenance and advance the protestant
religion abroad, which will be best done
by supporting the dignity and reverence
due to the best reformed protestant Church

at home.' On the basis of this Declaration the leading Puritan leaders were approached with offers of preferment, which were, however, declined with a single exception. REYNOLDS became Bishop of Norwich. The rest of the Puritans preferred to watch the progress of the Royal policy before committing themselves to a provisional acceptance of the settlement to which it was leading. The fate of the Declaration proved their wisdom. When it was proposed in the House of Commons to give it statutory force, the motion was rejected by 183 votes to 157. And it was observed that the King was nowise displeased with this result. Still, the hope of a moderate settlement had by no means perished.

STILLINGFLEET, whose 'Irenicum' appeared in a second edition in the course of the very year which witnessed the final rejection of the reconciling policy which it advocated, was the spokesman of many serious . Anglicans, when he urged the

relative   unimportance   of   ecclesiastical
polity :—

> ' The unity of the Church is   an
> unity of love and affection, and not a
> bare uniformity of practice or opinion.
> This latter is extremely desirable in
> a Church ; but as long as there are
> several ranks and sizes of men in it,
> very hardly attainable. . . . The only
> thing seeming to retard our peace is
> the controversy about Church-govern-
> ment, an unhappy controversy to us
> in England, if ever there were any
> in the world.   And the more unhappy
> in that our contentions about it have
> been so great, and yet so few of the
> multitudes engaged in it that have
> truly understood the matter they have
> so eagerly contended about.   For the
> state of the controversy, as it concerns
> us, lies not here, as it is generally
> mistaken, What form of Government
> comes the nearest to Apostolical prac-

tice ? but, *Whether any one individual form be founded so upon Divine Right, that all ages and Churches are bound unalterably to observe it ?* And certainly they who have espoused the most the interest of a *jus divinum* cannot yet but say, that if the opinion I maintain be true, it doth exceedingly conduce to a present settlement of the differences that are among us. For then all parties may retain their different opinions concerning the primitive form, and yet agree and pitch upon a form compounded of all together as the most suitable to the state and condition of the Church of GOD among us : that so the people's interest be secured by consent and, suffrage, which is the pretence of the congregational way, the due power of presbyteries asserted by their joint concurrence of the Bishop, as is laid down in that excellent model of the late incomparable Primate of Armagh, and the just honour and dignity of the Bishop asserted, as a very laudable and ancient constitution for preserving the peace and unity of the Church of GOD. . . . My main design throughout this whole treatise is to shew that there can be no argument drawn from any pretence of a Divine Right that may hinder men from consenting and yielding to such a form of government in the Church as may bear the greatest correspondency to the Primitive Church, and be most advantageously conducible to the peace, unity, and settlement of our divided Church. I plead not at all for any abuses or corruptions incident to the best form of Government through the corruption of men and times. Nay, I dare not harbour so low apprehensions of persons enjoying so great dignity and honour in the Church, that they will in any wise be unwilling of themselves to reduce

the Form of Church government
among us to its primitive state and
order, by retrenching all exorbitances
of power, and restoring those presbyteries which no law hath forbidden,
but only through disuse have been
laid aside. Whereby they will give
to the world that rare example of
self-denial and the highest Christian
prudence as may raise an honourable
opinion of them even amongst those
who have hitherto the most slighted
so ancient and venerable an order
in the Church of GOD, and thereby
become the repairers of those, otherwise irreparable, breaches in the
Church of GOD.'

STILLINGFLEET'S ' Irenicum ' was sub-
stantially the platform which the Puritans
were prepared to accept. Their contribution to the ecclesiastical settlement,
which all parties had professed to desire,
was the specific repudiation of presby-

terianism, and the acceptance of Episcopal Government, modified in certain particulars which everybody agreed were not essential, and which great numbers of religious people considered to be very desirable. They resented the description, 'presbyterians,' which their opponents were eager to fasten upon them. The preface to the second part of BAXTER's 'Nonconformist's Plea for Peace,' written in 1680, may be referred to as indicating the Puritan position. It is an indignant protest against the accusation of presbyterianism, as well as a very interesting statement of the course of events from the Puritan point of view. After reminding his readers that the Puritan ministers had originally agreed 'to desire or offer nothing for Church government but Archbishop USSHER's model of the primitive episcopal government,' and that 'when his Majesty would not grant us that model, nor the Bishops once treat about it,' they had agreed to

accept the scheme outlined in the Royal
Declaration, which 'offered and prescribed the episcopacy of England as
it stood with little alteration,' BAXTER
states of his own knowledge that presbyterianism 'out of London and Lancashire'
was practically non-existent, and that no
single congregation, other than the
tolerated Walloon congregations, existed
in London organised on the presbyterian
system.   He continues with characteristic
vehemence :—

> 'Set all this together and tell me
> whether it be likely that those men
> believe a life to come and a judge-
> ment of God, who would make King
> and People believe that Parliaments,
> Nonconforming Ministers, and their
> hearers are Presbyterians, and so
> many and so bad, as that King and
> Kingdom are in danger of them.'

In 1680, however, the issue had passed
from religion to politics, and the Noncon-

formists were denounced as disloyal to
the Monarchy, because they could not
echo the extravagant doctrines of
Monarchical Divine Right, which were
prevailing at the moment. But their
appeal from the new to the old Anglicans
was not less valid in respect to religion
than to politics. A change had passed
over the Anglican clergy in the interval
which separated the earlier Stuart period
from the later. The years of controversy
in exile had stamped a new character on
Anglicanism. Bishop CARLETON's bold
appeal to the success of the Church of
England as sufficient proof of Divine
approval, which had seemed sufficiently
valid when the Church was flourishing at
home and envied abroad, had lost validity
when the Church of England was represented only by crowds of exiles, wander-
ing in poverty from one foreign town to
another seeking the hospitality of the local
protestants. The controversy with Rome
had perforce taken a new urgency, and

received a new direction. It was no more possible to emphasise the national aspect of Anglicanism, for the nation had for the time being repudiated its Church. The appeal to antiquity still remained, and permitted an energetic argument against the papal prerogative. Accordingly it is to this period that we must ascribe that insistence on episcopacy as belonging to the very essence of Christianity, which at a later time found full expression in the writings of the Nonjurors, and has been within the last century revived and popularised by the Tractarians and their disciples. The Puritans had been so long out of touch with the Royalist clergy that they had not realised the change which had passed over them. The Restoration Settlement, which was undertaken with such copious professions of a desire for religious appeasement and comprehension, was finally carried through in the interest of a party which had become considerable during the civil troubles, and owed its dominating position, less to its own merits or consequence, than to the anti-Puritan reaction which effected the Restoration. It is a mistake to suppose that there was in the nation any general desire for the re-establishment of the ecclesiastical system which had existed before the wars. Dr. GARDINER has pointed out that there is no real evidence of anything of the kind :—

'There is little doubt that very considerable numbers, probably much more than a bare majority of the population, either did not care for ecclesiastical disputes at all, or at least did not care for them sufficiently to offer armed resistance to any form of Church-Government or Church-teaching likely to be established either by Parliament or by King. Yet all the evidence we possess shows the entire absence of any

popular desire amongst the laity outside the families of the Royalist
gentry and their immediate depen-
dents to bring back either episcopacy
or the Prayer Book. Riots there
occasionally were, but these were
riots because amusements had been
stopped, and especially because the
jollity of Christmas was forbidden,
not because the service in Church was
conducted in one way or another.'[1]

Dr. GARDINER insists that the Puritan
experiment failed, not on its ecclesiastical,
but on its moral side. It attempted to
impose on a nation the moral standard of
a religious community, and it scrupled not
to employ the crudest coercion in the
interest of its artificial and impracticable
morality :—

'It was no reaction against the
religious doctrines or ecclesiastical

[1] v. ' Oliver Cromwell,' p. 77.

institutions upheld by the Protector that brought about the destruction of his system of government. It is in the highest degree unlikely that a revolution would ever have taken place merely to restore episcopacy or the Book of Common Prayer. So far as the reaction was not directed against militarism, it was directed against the introduction into the political world of what appeared to be too high a standard of morality, a reaction which struck specially upon Puritanism, but which would have struck with as much force upon any other form of religion which, like that upheld by LAUD, called in the power of the State to enforce its claims.'[1]

The Prayer Book, never generally popular, had been out of use for twenty years. PEPYS observes on the failure of

[1] v. Ibid., p. 317.

a London congregation to make the
responses at Morning Prayer, and says
that in one City church the introduction
of the old but long-disused form of service
was received with unseemly demonstra-
tions of dislike from the congregation.
Had there been any genuine desire to
conciliate the Puritans, there was no reason
to fear any serious difficulty in the
parishes.   The authors of the Restoration
Settlement had a freer hand than the
Reformers of the sixteenth century.
Unfortunately the two men who were
mainly responsible for that Settlement,
CLARENDON and SHELDON, were resolved
to make no concessions, and they could
count on the relentless bigotry of the
Cavalier gentlemen who formed the
majority of the House of Commons, to
support them against the protests of
moderate men, and the evident reluctance
of the King.   It is to the honour of the
House of Lords that its influence was
cast on the side of equity and moderation.

While the Act of Uniformity was passing through Parliament, the Lords, in spite of the vehement opposition of the Bishops led by SHELDON, inserted a proviso which reserved to the King power to mitigate the effects of the measure, but even this concession to justice was immediately rejected by the Commons.

'Indeed,' says Mr. BATE in his excellent monograph, 'the Lords throughout took up the more conciliatory attitude, so much so that the Presbyterian ministers of Suffolk were said to have declared that the Lords' House was the House of the LORD, and so prayed for it. They endeavoured to amend the prescribed oaths, to secure for ejected ministers some portion of the living (as had been granted to the ejected royalist clergy), and to prevent the application of the bill to schoolmasters. On all points they had to give way to

the bitter intolerance of the Commons.
Thus on May 19, 1662, the bill
passed, and dissenters were left to
take what comfort they could from
the Chancellor's assurance that the
king would never suffer the weak to
undergo the punishment ordained for
the wicked.'[1]

The eviction of some two thousand
incumbents, and they unquestionably the
most earnest and successful, led to consequences of great moment which were,
perhaps, little contemplated by the leaders
of the re-established Church. Religious
dissent for the first time became both considerable and respected. For there could
be no doubt anywhere that the ejected
Puritans had been treated with gross
perfidy, and that they had preferred their
conscience to their interest. The Act of
Uniformity left them no choice between
retirement and infamy. The declaration,

[1] 'The Declaration of Indulgence, 1672,' p. 23.

which was now required of every clergyman
and schoolmaster, was so framed that no
conscientious Puritan could subscribe it
without degrading himself in his own
eyes, and in the eyes of his neighbours.
It ran thus :—

> ' I, A. B., do declare that it is not
> lawful, upon any pretence whatsoever,
> to take arms against the king; and
> that I do abhor that traitorous posi-
> tion of taking arms by his authority
> against his person or against those
> that are commissioned by him; and
> that I will conform to the liturgy of
> the Church of England, as it is
> now by law established; and I do
> declare that I do hold there lies no
> obligation upon me, or on any other
> person from the oath commonly
> called the Solemn League and
> Covenant, to endeavour any change
> or alteration of government either
> in Church or State; and that the

same was in itself an unlawful oath,
and imposed upon the subjects of
this realm against the known laws
and liberties of this kingdom.'

The Puritan who by this declaration
had immersed himself in the guilt of
perjury, had not yet sounded the depths
of his degradation. If, as was most
commonly the case, he had received his
ministry from other than episcopal hands,
he could only retain his benefice by
submitting himself for reordination, and
thus publicly branding his original ordination as invalid, and casting a slur of
suspicion upon all his ministrations. No
man of genuine piety could lend himself
to a procedure so profane. Thus the
issues, on which the fate of the Puritans
finally turned, were neither petty nor
obscure. The victims of the Act of
Uniformity were not ejected from the
National Church for disobedience to the
Prayer Book, but for refusing to lay

guilt on their consciences by uttering an evident falsehood, and for refusing to acquiesce in a sacrilegious farce. None, therefore, could pretend that they were separatists for slight cause, or question the motives of their compulsory dissent. They went forth to poverty, privation, and suffering. The victorious hierarchy was irreparably discredited, for not only was it clearly seen that the Puritans were the victims of cruelty and falseness, but it was soon found that their places could not easily or speedily be filled. The new incumbents were in too many cases men of small ability and inferior character: and numerous parishes were left for a long time without any spiritual provision before successors to the ejected Puritans could be found. 'Despite the earnest efforts of many bishops, the ministerial office continued to decline in public estimation. Before the close of the reign, the "contempt of the clergy" was a by-word.'[1]

[1] v. Bate, *l.c.* 34.

The Ejectment was the prelude to persecution. It could not but be so, for the ejected ministers constituted a new problem not easy of solution. They had been silenced, and thrust out, but they remained in the parishes, receiving from their devoted followers many significant tokens of respect and affection. Their principles in most cases held them back from formal separation. Many of them had been protagonists in the conflict with sectarianism, and they would not readily stultify the witness they had borne. Some of them still cherished the hope that their affliction was but temporary, and would be followed by some juster rearrangement making possible their ministry in the National Church :—

'When,' wrote BAXTER, the most illustrious of the ejected ministers, reviewing the history after an interval of seventeen years, 'the 1,800 or 2,000 Ministers were silenced, the

far greatest part of them forebore
all publick preaching, and only taught
some few in private at such hours as
hindered not the publick assemblies,
and many of them lived as private
men. To this day (1679) it is so
with many of the Nonconformists :
those that live where they find small
need of their preaching, or else have
no call or opportunity, and cannot
remove their dwellings, do hold no
assemblies, but as other men content
themselves to be auditors. Those
that live where are godly and peace-
able ministers, who yet need help,
do lead the people constantly to the
parish-churches, and teach them
themselves at other hours, and help
them from house to house : this is
ordinary in the countries [*i.e.*, coun-
ties], and even in London, with many
ministers that hold no assemblies, yea
many that were ejected out of City
parish churches.'

The transition from Nonconformity to Dissent or Separation was brought about by circumstances which certainly argued in the ejected ministers better motives than those of schismatic self-assertion. BAXTER continues his narrative :—

'It was the great and terrible plague in 1665 which made this change in their assembling and ministration. When the publick ministers foresook the City, and the rich left the poor to misery and death, and people looked every day for their last ; when they that heard a sermon one day were buried the next ; when Death had wakened the people to repentance, and a regard of their everlasting state, divers Nonconformable Ministers resolved to stay with them : they begged moneys out of the country for the poor and relieved them ; they got into the empty pulpits and preached to them. . . . And when GOD had blessed these men's faithful labours with the conversion of many souls (especially apprentices and young people) the experience so engaged their mutual affections, that the ministers resolved that they would live and die in such service as GOD had so blessed and preserved them in ; and their hearers resolved that they would not forsake their teachers. And thus the dreadful plague began that which now so much offendeth men, as a dangerous Schism.'

The Plague was quickly followed by the Fire, and this calamity also had its effect on the procedure of the Nonconformists :—

' When some men out of excessive caution were ready to think that when that plague had ceased (having killed about an hundred thousand) the Ministers should lay by that publick work, and retire again into

secret corners, God confuted them
by His next dreadful judgment,
burning down the city the next year,
1666. So that there were neither
churches to go to, nor ministers in
the parishes to preach, nor rich men
to maintain them : and could any
soul that hated not Christ and men's
salvation, have wished the Nonconformists then to desert the miserable
people? . . . These two great and
notorious calamities succeeding in
these two dreadful years, 1665, 1666,
calling the Nonconformable Ministers
out of their retirements, and latitant
and silent state, resolved them to
serve God more diligently and openly
than they had done, whatever it cost
them ; and many country ministers
were awakened to the like by the
examples of those in London, though
yet a great number who are in places
of less need, or not called out as
aforesaid, still lie much silent.'

Here follows in BAXTER'S narrative a paragraph printed in capital letters, in order to arrest the reader's eye, and impress him with a sense of its terrible significance, which sets in contrast with the pastoral zeal of the ejected Ministers, the shameless cruelty of their persecutors. It runs thus :—

'While the dreadful fire was wasting London and other corporations, the Parliament and Bishops were at Oxford, making an Oath to drive all Nonconformists above five miles from all cities and corporations that send Burgesses to Parliament, and all all other places wherever they had preached since the Act of Oblivion. So that had they obeyed the Laws, London had been deserted in the plague and in the ruins, and few people suffered publicly to worship GOD.'[1]

[1] v. 'The Nonconformist's Plea for Peace,' pp. 235–240 (London, 1679).

The evident leadings of Providence, for so the Puritans could not but interpret the facts of their experience, had brought them into the situation of dissenters, and the policy of the government, which necessarily they regarded as primarily that of the National Church, forced them to attach increasing importance to the objections which they had always felt to certain parts of the Established System. Thus formal separation went hand-in-hand with deepening aversion. The hardships to which they were subjected neither widened their outlook, nor sweetened their temper. When the nightmare of persecution passed, and once more an opportunity seemed to present itself for restoring the broken unity of English Religion, it was found that there no longer existed among the Puritans any adequate desire to return to the National System, or any strong wish to escape from the dubious situation in which they stood. Comprehension, possible in 1660, had ceased to be possible in 1689. Its place was taken by the policy of Toleration, a policy which implied a lowering of the religious ideal, as well as a triumph of civic good sense. Sectarianism prevailed alike in the National Church, and in the tolerated Sects, and the religious unity of the English people was destroyed perhaps for ever.

Puritanism has survived less in the dissenters, who have long emerged from the relative inferiority of 'Toleration' to the position of complete religious equality, and are now really, in a true sense, 'established churches,' worshipping alongside of the historical 'National Church,' than in certain distinctive features of English religion—its comparative indifference to religious observances, its almost fanatical dislike of the Roman Church, its exaltation of the Bible, its religious insularity, its Sabbatarian sentiment, above all, the deep division running right across the Established Church between Evangelical and Sacerdotal Christianity.

THE HUGUENOT CHURCH OF CANTERBURY

Preached in the Crypt of Canterbury Cathedral on the 6th Sunday after Trinity, being the 364th anniversary of the Founding of the Church by the French and Walloon refugees.

THE HUGUENOT CHURCH OF
CANTERBURY

'God chose the weak things of the world, that He might put to shame the things that are strong.'—
I CORINTHIANS i. 27.

NEARLY 350 years have passed since the refugees from France and the Netherlands sought the hospitality of this city, and were welcomed here as fellow-believers. In the year 1550 they were established in possession of the Crypt of Canterbury Cathedral by the grant of KING EDWARD VI., and there they and their descendants have worshipped through successive generations until this day, when we have gathered together to commemorate their original settlement. In no unreal sense it may be said of the Huguenots and Walloons that they saved the Reformation when its fortunes were desperate, saved it by their unconquerable courage and by their immense sufferings, saved it by the martyrdom of COLIGNY, by the genius of CALVIN, and by the steadfast courage of WILLIAM THE SILENT. The wheel of destiny has brought such dramatic changes, that we to-day can hardly realise the discrepancy of resources which marked that vital conflict in which the Massacre of St. Bartholomew, and the still more sanguinary cruelties of ALVA were incidents, and from which the Huguenot Church of Canterbury was born. The balance of political power has moved from the Latin to the English and German peoples, from the Governments which accept the authority of the Roman papacy to those which repudiate it. It is not easy for us to realise the situation of

Europe when the mighty conflict of the Reformation began. Then the overwhelming weight of political power was opposed to the Reformers. When the young son of HENRY VIII. ascended the throne of England, he was the only monarch of importance who stood for the Reformation, and none could be quite sure, with the experiences of his father's reign fresh in mind, whether indeed he would finally stand for it, and would not rather consult his obvious interest by making his peace with the Emperor. When we consider the general acceptance of the monstrous method of murder and massacre by the Roman Catholic Powers, we must remember that, in the actual circumstances of the time, it did not seem improbable that by that means the Reformation might be totally and speedily suppressed. This circumstance may mitigate our astonishment, but it cannot lessen our disgust at the open and eager approval which that method received from the leaders of the Roman Catholic Church. Lord ACTON's remarkable essay on the Massacre of St. Bartholomew, recently published in the volume entitled 'The History of Freedom,' should be studied by every one who would grasp the full significance of that terrible episode. Himself a devout Roman Catholic, as well as an erudite and accomplished historian, Lord ACTON's verdict on the conduct of the Roman Church is peculiarly weighty.

2. The intolerance which banished from the soil of France so many thousands of French Protestants, amid scenes of heart-rending cruelty, brought a curse on that country so manifest that it leaps to the eyes of the historian. Not only were the moral resources of the nation depleted by the withdrawal of its most virile and conscientious members, but the exiles carried away with them to their new homes in England and Prussia much mechanical skill and many valuable industries. In the political sphere we

may trace the ill consequences of the persecutions in the unwholesome and unchecked development of Absolutism. The French Revolution was latent in the policy which violently suppressed the French Reformation ; and the unhappy discord between Church and State in France, which is at the present time the salient feature of its internal situation, is directly traceable to the crimes and follies of the sixteenth and seventeenth centuries.

3. This Huguenot Church of Canterbury is, then, the creation of religious intolerance, a standing monument of a policy which once commended itself to the Statesmen of Europe, a conspicuous illustration of a principle which once ruled the consciences and chilled the sympathies of Christian men. Its presence here in the crypt of the great cathedral points another moral. Protestantism stands and falls with the principle of Private Judgment and with the policy of Religious

Liberty. It is the case that Protestants were slow to realise the full meaning of the position which they adopted, that they were inconsistent, that they were slow to abandon the habits which centuries had bound into their minds, that their record is stained by many scandals. Persecution was not confined to Roman Catholics. Fanaticism is of no creed, and of all Churches. Only three years after the Huguenots were established in the crypt, SERVETUS was burned at Geneva with the general approval of Protestants throughout Europe. Archbishop ABBOT insisted on the burning of two unhappy heretics at Smithfield in 1614, and gave his approval to the use of torture. Archbishop USSHER opposed the toleration of the Roman Catholic Religion in Ireland. The earliest advocates of religious toleration were the despised sectaries who gathered at Amsterdam, or ventured across the stormy Atlantic to lay the foundations of the American Republic;

and even they could not hold to their principles when once the power to persecute came into their hands. Only the Quakers have a clean record in this respect. They have never persecuted, or justified persecution. Still, with so much inconsistency on the part of individuals, so much cruelty in the policy of Protestant States and Churches, it remains the case that Protestantism is inherently inconsistent with religious intolerance, and that within the Protestant sphere religious liberty has established itself as the proper consequence of Protestant principles. From the first the difference was felt. Make the most of the scandals of Protestant intolerance, and you cannot pretend that they approach in magnitude and horror the persecutions of the Roman Church. It is an insult to human intelligence to pretend that the treatment of Roman Catholics by QUEEN ELIZABETH was on a level with that of Protestants by

QUEEN MARY, or that persecution has played in the history of Protestant States a *rôle* comparable with that which it played up to quite recent times in Roman Catholic communities. The reason lies in the circumstance that while Protestant principles disallow religious intolerance, Roman Catholic principles require it. The comparative absence of persecution in our own age is due, not to any change of Roman Catholic theory, but to lack of power to apply the old theory to modern life. In order to prevent any misunderstanding on the point, we have the attempt to enforce the 'Ne Temere' decree respecting mixed marriages actually being made both in Ireland and in Canada at the present time. Less publicly scandalous, but perhaps even more reprehensible, has been the violent suppression of the Modernist Movement within the Roman Catholic Church. While, then, the old enemy against which the Huguenots fought with such noble courage still confronts us, we may well treasure so famous a monument of their conflict as this Church presents.

4. But apart from this general interest a Huguenot Church worshipping in this place from the very beginning of the Reformation has a special value to English Churchmen. It comes to us from a time in which the National Church of England was in close fellowship with the other Reformed Churches, and it illustrates the position which in those days was common to all Protestants, that the essentials of Christianity are not to be found in the region of external system, but in a common faith. All the Reformed Churches came into existence as the consequence of a revolt against the ancient and established system of the Medieval Church. All the Reformers, English and continental alike, had to face the question, Whether they could rightly insist on their own per-

ceptions of truth against the authoritative
decisions of the Church? They often
used ambiguous language ; often caught
up theories, whether of the Church or
of the Nation, which obscured the issue ;
sometimes, perhaps, were not able to
realise the meaning of the decisions they
took ; yet, broadly, the position was clear
enough when the constituted authorities
of the Western Church, the hierarchy
and the papacy as its Divinely constituted
organ, had spoken formally and decisively
in condemnation of the reforming movement. What authority should men
accept in religion? What did they
really mean by truth? When LUTHER
burned the Pope's Bull of excommunication, there could be no mistaking his
attitude. He repudiated the claim of
the pope, that is, of the constituted
ecclesiastical system, to declare what was
truth, and thus to determine the belief
of a Christian man. He claimed to have
a higher authority within himself. He

adopted towards the Church authority precisely the same position as that which St. Peter adopted towards the Sanhedrin, ' *We must obey God rather than men* '; and he assumed that the conviction of truth which he had formed was rightly described as God's Word to him. That is what is meant by Private Judgment. In the last result the decision what is or is not true must be made by every man for himself. This is at once the glory and the burden of manhood, its incommunicable responsibility, and its unique greatness. Truth is not to be identified with the decision of an external authority, but has its sanctions within the individual conscience, and by the Divine right of its own inherent excellence commands the acceptance of true men. Knowledge is relative, but truth is in this sense absolute that its claim to be received is never less than Divine, and its title to be received is never for one instant doubtful. Therefore, whenever truth is perceived,

there emerges for every man who per-
ceives it the crucial issue of religion.
Not to accept the truth which we
perceive is to play the traitor to our own
best selves, and to exchange the service
of the GOD of Truth for that of the Father
of Lies. But such acceptance may bring
us into conflict with great vested interests
of ancient and powerful falsehood.
Then arises the demand for faith. The
near, present, insistent fact claims us by
the intelligible pleas of our evident
material interest. The remote, unseen,
unarmoured truth has no other pleas
than those which the conscience feels,
and the reason owns. That was the
issue which faced the Reformers ; that
was the conflict in which the Martyrs
died. They valued liberty of thought
and worship so highly that for its sake
they endured willingly every earthly
disaster. '*With a great sum*' they
obtained their freedom, for they knew
full well,

' There is a bondage worse, far worse, to bear
    Than his who breathes, by roof, and floor, and
        wall
    Pent in, a Tyrant's solitary Thrall:
    'Tis his who walks about in the open air,
    One of a Nation who, henceforth, must wear
    Their fetters in their souls.'

This Church of the Martyrs is a standing witness to the faith which overcame the world, the faith in the unseen. These exiles for conscience' sake, whose memorials are about us here, like MOSES, when he turned his back on the Court of PHARAOH and the pleasures of Egypt, ' *endured as seeing Him who is invisible.*'

5. We are ourselves witnesses of the power of their faith, for we enjoy the fruits of its triumph. I adverted just now to the superiority of physical force which lay with the persecutors of the Huguenots. At the Reformation, and, at least in the case of the Protestants of France and the Netherlands, throughout the century which followed, the battle for religious liberty,

for the right of Private Judgment, for
the truth as GOD had shown it to the
individual, was fought against terrible
odds. Writing at the very end of the
sixteenth century, Sir EDWIN SANDYS,
when he reviewed the relative strength of
the friends and foes of the Reformation,
found a great superiority in the latter.
They were more numerous, more civilised,
more wealthy, more united. Protestants
were inferior in every element of success.
Yet we know now that such was the
inherent vigour of freedom, such the
dynamic force of religious conviction,
that all disadvantages were finally overcome, and the triumph of the Reformation
finally established. As we review the conflict, and realise the magnitude of the
victory, we share the reverent amazement with which ST. PAUL beheld
the first conquests of Christianity : ' *God
chose the foolish things of the world, that
He might put to shame them that are wise ;
and God chose the weak things of the world,*

*that He might put to shame the things that
are strong ; and the base things of the world,
and the things that are despised, did God
choose, yea, and the things that are not,
that He might bring to nought the things
that are : that no flesh should glory before
God.'* The seeming success of the policy
of persecution, which stained the annals of
France with the massacre of 1572, and
the crowning perfidy of 1685, became
ministerial to the lasting establishment of
religious liberty in other lands : and the
descendants of the exiles who bore the
brunt of the great conflict and carried
to these shores the faith which no
extremity of oppression could make
them betray, and the hopes which no
lengths of calamity could make them
abandon, have a sacred title to our
sympathy and, if need be, to our support,
as they maintain here the sacred traditions
of that age of sorrow and suffering.

6. Are there any among us who would
suggest that the memory of the heroic

past might be suffered to fade : that the victory of liberty has been so firmly secured that there is no adequate justification for recalling the exasperations of the conflict in which it was gained : that the old bad tyrannous fallacies of bigotry have lost their hold over men's minds, and could never again menace the happiness and self-respect of civilised men ? Give me leave to point out to them that the ancient' conflict must continue, albeit in novel forms, so long as human nature remains what it is : that there are no signs that the moral of its historic failures has been learned by the Church of Rome : that there are many indications that the spirit of intolerance has extended from the religious to the political and economic spheres : that the rights of the individual conscience never stood in more urgent need of vigilant championship than in these days of organised industry, and great centralised communities.

The salient feature of modern politics is

the new importance of the working classes. This, we are told, is to be the character of the social revolution which is visibly dawning on the western world—the triumph of the ideas, and the endorsement of the ideals of the artisans. Is it sufficiently remembered that there is a relatively feeble sense of individuality among the working classes? The circumstances in which they live and work may develop many admirable qualities, but they are not favourable to this master-quality, which is the key to true human development, individual self-respect. Nothing is more charged with sinister promise than the tyrannous contempt for individual rights which marks the organisations of working men. The Catholic Church of Labour will be not less ready to use coercion in the interest of its creed than the Catholic Church of CHRIST : and in the future the demand for the virile and heroic qualities which created Protestantism, will not be less than in the past. The tyrannies of the world change their names and forms, but never their character. There is a despotism of wealth as well as of political power : a persecution by the civilised agents of defamation and boycott, as well as by the crude ancient methods of the sword and stake. The world to-day has its martyrs, and, if I read aright the signs of the times, will have them in greater number in the coming age. Therefore we cannot afford to suffer any factor of modern life which is friendly to personal independence to decline, or permit any tradition from the past which stimulates personal self-respect to fail. Here in this little Huguenot Church, nestling in its ancient refuge in the crypt of Canterbury Cathedral, is precisely such a factor, and the embodiment of such a tradition. Economic changes have reduced its numbers, but withdrawn nothing of its moral significance. If I might be permitted to address myself to those citizens of Canterbury, who are themselves connected by hereditary ties

with the Huguenot exiles, who founded
this Church, I would beg of them to
recognise an honourable responsibility for
its well-being. They will render good
service to this famous and beautiful City if
they cherish with loving solicitude this
precious relic from the past, and enable it
to bear its high and necessary witness in
our modern life. Canterbury is rich
beyond most other cities in monuments
and memories, but to the informed and
considering visitor there is, perhaps, no
monument more sacred, no memory more
inspiring, than these which fill with solemn
interest the crypt of the Cathedral.

7. To the National Church of England,
which welcomed the French and Walloon
refugees 364 years ago, this Church has
an interest and a value which cannot be
exaggerated. If it be the case—and
can it be denied that it is ?—that there are
at the present time tendencies within the
Church of England which belittle and even
repudiate the principles of the Reforma-

tion, and would build again in this country
the fabric of ancient religious errors, which
our Fathers at the peril of their lives over-
threw, then it cannot be a small thing that
we should have in our midst, nay in the
very heart of our system, a living demon-
stration of our true character as a
Reformed Church. Nay; there is a
deeper truth suggested, one which holds
not merely of every Reformed Church,
but of the Christian Church in its entirety,
so far as in any measure it remains true to
its spiritual allegiance, and is in fact as
well as in name a Church of CHRIST.
This place for us is steeped in symbolism.
CANTERBURY CATHEDRAL, rising in peer-
less beauty out of the old City, which it
seems to hallow and ennoble, filled with
the memorials of a national past which
runs back across the centuries into the
twilight of a remote antiquity, echoing
daily the solemn liturgical worship of a
great National Church, and withal cherish-
ing in the dark recesses of the crypt, as it

were within its very foundations, a simpler worship, fashioned in times of desperate trial, the workmanship of martyrs and exiles, eloquent at every point of affliction and conflict, is no inadequate symbol of the Christian Church itself. At the root of all the glorious expressions of faith in literature, in art, in history, there are the stern simple truths for which men have fought and died, the principles and convictions which inspire all genuine Christian effort, the faith which overcomes the world.

In many forms, and in widely varying circumstances, GOD puts His children to the test. In halcyon days of prosperity we may easily forget the inexorable and unchanging conditions of liberty, but when the dark times come, alike for nations and for individuals, those forgotten conditions emerge into threatening prominence. '*What shall a man give in exchange for his soul? What shall it profit a man if he gain the whole world and lose or forfeit his own self?*'—these questions claim their answer from all of us sooner or later. O then, when to our Nation or to ourselves the solemn issue comes, and we must face it, GOD grant that the Spirit of the Martyrs, whom we recall with loving homage to-day, may be ours, and we in our turn may be found faithful to our trust!

RICHARD BUSBY

Preached in Westminster Abbey on September
23, 1906

RICHARD BUSBY

BORN SEPTEMBER 22, 1606
DIED APRIL 6, 1695

'The righteous shall be had in everlasting remembrance.'—PSALM cxii. 6.

TWO anniversaries of general interest fell within the week that has just ended, and both of them have a particular interest for us, who live and work in this place. Just three hundred years have elapsed since, on September 22, 1606, RICHARD BUSBY was born in the parish of Lutton in Lincolnshire. Just one hundred and ninety - seven years ago on September 18, 1709, SAMUEL JOHNSON first saw the light in Lichfield. Both the great Schoolmaster and the great Lexicographer lie buried within these walls. Perhaps there are few tombs more reverently regarded here than theirs. The two men belonged to the same vigorous middle class of society, rather on its lower side where it merges in the vast army of manual labourers, than on its upper where it passes into the smaller literary and leisured class. Both were born into poor homes, and had to enter on the struggle of life without the doubtful advantage of inherited wealth. Both men came of a religious stock, religious in the old English Churchman's sense fashioned by the greater Elizabethans and revived, though on narrower lines, after the Great Rebellion. Both were the sons of Churchwardens, and notable among their contemporaries for their severe and unyielding Churchmanship. Both were Oxford men, and conspicuous examples of the strength, and perhaps also of the limitations, of the educational methods of their time. Both men impressed their contemporaries wonderfully, being indeed universally allowed to be the most striking and original personalities of their time. The influence of both men was pre-eminently moral, and had its root in a deep and simple piety. Both men were magnanimously benevolent, and though rough and caustic in speech and almost brutally contemptuous of everything which seemed to them unreal or effeminate, very tender-hearted and unworldly. Not to pursue the parallel to tiresome lengths, it must suffice to say that both men illustrated the triumph of character. Of RICHARD BUSBY I shall take leave to speak rather more particularly, because he belongs to Westminster in a degree which is quite unique.

Very soon after his birth his father removed from Lincolnshire to Westminster, where his own long life of 89 years was to be spent. Of his poverty we have an interesting indication in the fact, recorded in the churchwardens' accounts

of St. Margaret's, Westminster, that the
vestry of that parish voted the money
needed for his graduation at Oxford as
Bachelor of Arts in 1628, and as Master
three years later. It is not, perhaps,
generally known that the same accounts
record his repayment of the money thus
given to him. In the year 1649 the
Churchwardens acknowledge the receipt of
£11 13s. 4d. 'of Mr. RICHARD BUSBY, it
having formerly been disbursed for his
use . . . which so soon as it was made
known to him, he immediately repaid it.'
At that time BUSBY had been Headmaster
of Westminster School for eleven years,
and he was destined to hold his office
for forty-six more. During that long
headmastership of fifty-seven years, he
accumulated a large property, and, being
unmarried and without relations who had
any claim on him, he bestowed the whole
of it in good works. His will is a long
enumeration of religious and benevolent
purposes. He is, perhaps, the most con-

spicuous example that age affords of Lord
BACON's dictum about the advantage of
the single life from the point of view of
the public interest. 'Certainly the best
works, and of greatest merit for the
public, have proceeded from the unmarried
or childless men, which both in affection
and means have married and endowed
the public.' BUSBY'S zeal for education
coloured his benefactions. At Westminster, at Oxford, at Willen, where his
estate lay, at Lutton, where he was born,
he gave money, and bequeathed it, for
the promotion of education, and especially
of religious education. It would seem, if
we may indulge conjecture, that two circumstances of his own experience had
sunk deeply into his mind. He had lived
through the stormy period of the Commonwealth, and had observed with alarm and
disgust the wild and sometimes dangerous
vagaries of religious opinion which marked
the sectaries, and he had known in himself
the inestimable advantages of an early,

solid, and religious training.   Accordingly
his principal concern was to ground boys
in the principles of religion, and to provide
for them the opportunities of education.
BUSBY was emphatically a man of action,
not a man of ideas.   Neither his great
contemporary, MILTON, who was keeping
school in the City at the time, and criti-
cising with his deep illuminating wisdom
the traditional didactic methods which
BUSBY, and JOHNSON afterwards, cham-
pioned, nor his own famous pupil, LOCKE,
would have received from him much
approval.   His fondness for the rod,
exaggerated no doubt by tradition, was
only one among many indications of his
thoroughgoing conservatism in educational method.   ' His contempt of the
professional scholar '—observes our school
historian, in his well-known excellent
' Annals of Westminster School '—' was
outdone by his contempt for the educational amateur.'   But this judgment is,
perhaps, in some degree modified by the

statement that 'he was always alive to new knowledge, and always seeking fresh subjects of instruction.'[1]   BUSBY'S eminence as a schoolmaster, however, did not lie in the region of didactic experiment or reform, but in that of practical work. '*The glory of fathers is their children*' is a proverb of Scripture which is notably illustrated by the career of a teacher. The measure of his success, and the proof of his distinction, are found in the disciples whom he trains, and fills with his spirit.   Perhaps no schoolmaster ever trained so many men famous in many categories of fame as BUSBY.   In the seventeenth century the higher intellect of the nation ran in clerical channels as never since, and it is said that no less than sixteen Bishops at one time were old scholars of BUSBY.   This astonishing success, which raised Westminster School to the primacy among the public schools of the

[1] v. 'Annals of Westminster School,' by John Sergeaunt, p. 113 f. (Methuen and Co., 1898).

time, was due to the contagious influence of a masterful and lofty character. It was not only boys who felt and responded to this influence, though naturally they were most powerfully affected. The mere fact that BUSBY was allowed to retain his office throughout the interregnum, in spite of his strong and openly-confessed adhesion to the cause of Church and King, is perhaps the strongest evidence of the impression he made upon his contemporaries, while it certainly reflects great credit on the dominant Puritans, whose genuine zeal for education overcame the prejudices of creed and the passions of political party. When we inquire wherein this remarkable personal influence consisted, we cannot be mistaken in answering that it arose mainly from BUSBY's ability to arouse and enlist the conscience of his pupils. In spite of his severity he was felt to be just, and his firm Churchmanship was conditioned by a genuine respect for conscientious scruples, rare indeed among his contemporaries and co-religionists. The well-known Nonconformist, PHILIP HENRY, has left on record the impression made on him by the great Headmaster. At the request of the boy's mother BUSBY had allowed him to be absent from school daily from seven to eight in the morning, in order that he might attend the sermons then preached in the Abbey by a rota of Puritan divines, and every Thursday he says that his mother 'took him also to Mr. THO. CASE, his lecture at St. Martin's Church, and every monthly Fast to St. Margaret's, Westminster, which was our Parish Church where preacht the ablest men of England before the then House of Commons.' He goes on to relate the only occasion on which he was flogged. He told a lie, and was properly punished for it :—

> 'Mr. BUSBY turn'd his eye towards me and said καὶ σὺ τέκνον, and whipt mee, which was the only time

I felt the weight of his hand, and I deserv'd it. Hee appointed me also a Penitential copy of Latin verses which I made and brought him, and then hee gave mee sixpence and received mee again into his favor. April 14th (or yer. abouts) 1647. The LORD was graciously pleased to bring me home effectually to Himself by ye means of my Schoolmaster Mr. RICHARD BUSBY at the time of ye solemne preparation for ye Communion then observ'd. The LORD recompense it a thousand fold into his bosome. I hope I shal never forget. There had been Treatyes before between my soul and JESUS with some overtures towards Him, but then, then I think it was that the match was made.' [1]

When the Act of Uniformity compelled

[1] Quoted in the 'Memoir of Richard Busby, D.D.,' by G. F. Russell Barker, pp. 83, 85 (Lawrence and Bullen, 1895).

the Puritan clergy to decide whether they would repudiate their Presbyterian Orders, or resign their benefices, PHILIP HENRY was among the Nonconformists. ' BUSBY asked him some time afterwards, "Prythee, child, what made thee a nonconformist?" His answer was, " Truly, Sir, you made me one, for you taught me those things that hindered me from conforming."' It is impossible to imagine a nobler tribute to the religious teaching which BUSBY had given his boys. He had not succeeded in making the little Puritan an Anglican, but he had so stamped on his mind the sanctity and sovereignty of conscience, that, when the great trial came to him, which in some form or other comes to all men, and he had to make his choice between his worldly prospects and his loyalty to conscience, he unhesitatingly cast in his lot with the latter.

BUSBY was, as we have said, a strong Churchman and Loyalist, but these characters were not inconsistent with his

submission to the ruling powers during
the Commonwealth, nor did they restrain
him from subscribing both the Covenant
and the Engagement. It is one of the
strangest facts about his career that no
stigma appears to have rested on him in
any quarter on this account. His position
was as secure under the reigning Puritans,
as under the restored Monarchy. He
walked in procession in Westminster
Abbey at the funeral of OLIVER, and he
carried the Ampulla two years later at
the Coronation of CHARLES. The explanation, so far as there is any, seems
to lie in his devotion to his profession.
He was before all things, and everybody
understood the fact, a schoolmaster, and
he acquiesced as a matter of course in the
political arrangements of the country so
long as they did not interfere with his
teaching work. Within that sphere he
would brook no interference. Outside
that sphere he did not interfere. Men
recognised and chafed against his jealousy

of interference, but perforce they acknow-
ledged his enthusiasm and his good faith.
His name became symbolic of arbitrary
but righteous authority. '*The Chair
behaves himself like a Busby amongst so
many school-boys, as some say,*' notes
THOMAS BURTON in his Parliamentary
Diary, and he adds significantly that '*he
takes a little too much on him, but
grandly.*' The sentence would not,
perhaps, be wholly inappropriate as a
description of BUSBY's didactic method.
'*He took too much upon him, but grandly.*'
The circumstances of a schoolmaster's life
undoubtedly tend to encourage an exalted
estimate of one's own importance, and of
course we all know that the pedagogue
has become proverbial for a special type
of professional vanity. Every career has
its distinctive faults, and the schoolmaster
enjoys no exception from the general law.
Yet a measure of undue self-importance
is but a small price for such genuine
exaltation of thought as that which

inspired BUSBY'S performance of duty. I
would venture respectfully to offer his
example to the attentive study of the
noble profession which he adorned and
raised in the public estimation. Since the
seventeenth century, the schoolmaster's
status in society has been greatly improved. It would no longer be reasonable to complain, as BUSBY'S famous
pupil, SOUTH (whose monument rises at
the foot of his master's, and who shared
with him the distinction of being a
Prebendary of this Church), could justly
complain, that schoolmasters were not
treated with due regard :—

    ' I know not how it comes to pass,'
he said in one of his sermons, ' that
this honourable employment should
find so little respect (as experience
shows it does) from too many in the
world. For there is no profession
which has, or can have, a greater
influence upon the public. School-

masters have a negative upon the
peace and welfare of the kingdom.
They are indeed the great deposi-
tories and trustees of the peace of it
as having the growing hopes and
fears of the nation in their hands.
For generally, subjects are and will
be such as they breed them. So
that I look upon an able, well-
principled schoolmaster as one of
the most meritorious subjects in any
prince's dominions that can be ; and
every such school, under such a
master, as a seminary of loyalty and
a nursery of allegiance.'

South goes on to speak of the methods
by which schoolmasters should fulfil their
great function in the nation :—

    ' But now, if their power is so
great and their influence so strong,
surely it concerns them to use it to
the utmost for the benefit of their

country. And for this purpose let them fix this as an eternal rule or principle in the instruction of youth ; *that care is to be had of their manners in the first place, and of their learning in the next.* And here, as the foundation and ground-work of all morality let youth be taught betimes to obey, and to know that the very relation between teacher and learner imports superiority and subjection.'

South warns schoolmasters against that excessive severity which was common in the schools of the time, and which indeed was supposed to find special favour with Busby, though the mere circumstance that this warning should find a place in a sermon which contains a warm eulogy of Westminster School, and was originally intended to have been preached in this church, and presumably in Busby's presence, goes far to show that the supposition is without real ground. Nothing could be wiser than this counsel to schoolmasters, and it is counsel which can never lose its relevance :—

> ' Let them remember that excellent and never-to-be-forgotten advice, *that boys will be men ;* and that the memory of all base usage will sink so deep into, and grow up so inseparably with them, that it will not be so much as in their power ever to forget it. For though indeed schoolmasters are a sort of kings, yet they cannot always pass such acts of oblivion as shall operate upon their scholars, or perhaps, in all things indemnify themselves.'

SOUTH warns against 'cowing and depressing' children 'with scoffs and contumelies,' and insists that in all punishments it must be made to appear 'that the person is loved while his fault is punished; nay, that one is punished only out of love to the other.' I shall adopt for myself as my excuse for inflicting these quotations on you the plea, which the great orator originally advanced for himself :—

'These things I thought fit to remark about the education and educators of youth in general, not that I have any thoughts or desires of invading their province; but possibly a stander-by may sometimes look as far into the game as he who plays it; and perhaps with no less judgment, because with much less concern.' [1]

The schoolmaster, like the clergyman, ought to lie outside the sphere of party politics just because in both cases the work to be done demands for its due

[1] v. Sermons, vol. iii. p. 83 f.

fulfilment the confidence of the public, apart from which that liberty of action, which is indispensable for both, cannot be conceded. You must trust the school-master, and you must trust the clergyman, but no sane man will trust those whom he has good reason for suspecting, and you may be sure that such reasons will not be lacking if the schoolmaster or the clergy-man sinks to be the parasite of party and the tool of faction.

Schoolmasters have a primary interest in the record of one who was a great schoolmaster, but BUSBY was also a great citizen, and as such I shall take leave to commend his example to those also who are not schoolmasters. Let me fasten on but two features of his citizenship. First of all consider his benefactions to the public. He had received much from others. As a KING'S SCHOLAR of Westminster, and as a Student of Christ Church, he had been educated by means of the ancient endowments of

'Founders and Benefactors.' He had
received help, as I reminded you, from
the Vestry of St. Margaret's. BUSBY was
no thankless beneficiary, but rejoiced to
repay what he had received in ampler
measure. Every institution, and every
locality whereby he had benefited, was
the better for the fact. He gave back
with generosity more than he had taken.
In this respect he sets an example which
the men of our time specially need to
learn. How few they are in any generation who feel any personal obligation
attaching to the endowments which they
enjoy! What ought to be received as a
free gift is too often taken as a right, and
as no gratitude is felt, so no return is
made. In this respect I think we are
inferior to our fathers. Who now in his
prosperity takes thought for his native
village, or for the profession in which he
has gained wealth and honour, or for the
school where the foundations of his
success were laid, or for the college which

first opened for him the doors to a career? There are exceptions which all will call to mind, and these perhaps conceal the general ingratitude. Consider next BUSBY's treatment of his property. He came to be comparatively a rich man, and his handling of his property is worthy the attention of rich men, especially of men who have gained riches. He did not make haste to retire from work. Idleness and display had no attractions for him. He did not spend his wealth on selfish objects, becoming I do not say a profligate (for such a character is inconceivable in connection with a man of his strong and religious type), but a mere collector of pictures, or books, or gems, a dilettantist, who 'killed the impracticable hours' by self-amusement with some hobby. BUSBY's money was honourably earned, and it was responsibly expended. In his hands property was moralised; his ownership was clearly to the general advantage. These are days when the manner in which

wealth is expended is only less important,
if it is less important, than the way in
which wealth is acquired, for the conscience
of mankind is becoming increasingly
restive on the subject of property. The
gross and well-nigh intolerable inequalities
of civilised society are weighing on men's
hearts, and the spectacle of vast unearned
wealth being squandered in unworthy
indulgence is moving resentments so deep
that they must some day find adequate
expression in action. There are audible
mutterings as to the advancing danger of
Socialism, and a sense of insecurity is
spreading amongst us. The strongest
argument for Socialism is not any provided by its professed advocates, but that
which the owners of Wealth are daily
offering ; I mean, the argument from the
scandals of individual ownership, the
abuse of wealth to selfish and even abominable purposes. I speak of the wealthy,
but they are, when all is said, but a small
section of the property-owners. The

obligation to earn honestly and spend un-
selfishly rests on all of us alike.

There is something to my mind very
solemn and inspiring in the fact that after
so many years—it is 300 since RICHARD
BUSBY was born in the little Lincolnshire
parish, which has piously honoured his
memory by sending a wreath to be placed
on his tomb—I say there is something
very solemn and inspiring about the fact
that after all these years we should be
able to exult in the virtues, and uphold
the example, of this good man. We
recall the words of the old Psalmist, who
himself also had watched the courses of
human lives : '*Well is it with the man
that dealeth graciously and lendeth: he
shall maintain his cause in judgment.
For he shall never be moved; the righteous
shall be had in everlasting remembrance.*'
And if we must confess that there is much
goodness in this world which misses recognition, and that many heroes and saints
are among those who have no memorial,

and to the generations that follow them, are as if they had never been, yet we know that this is but a superficial view of the facts. Nothing good ever really fails of its blessing and of its recompense. '*For*,' as the great Apostle, himself a Martyr and the most honoured of the Saints, said, ' *Whether we live, we live unto the Lord ; or whether we die, we die unto the Lord : whether we live therefore, or die, we are the Lord's.*'

THE MORAL OF A GREAT FAILURE

Preached to the University of Cambridge on the
Fifth Sunday after Easter, May 12, 1912.

THE MORAL OF A GREAT FAILURE

The wrath of man worketh not the righteousness of God.—JAMES i. 20.

IN the month of May, A.D. 1662, just 250 years ago, the Royal Assent was given to a measure which has affected profoundly the life of the English people, and the fortunes of the English Church. The Act of Uniformity must be regarded as one of the most fruitful achievements of the legislator's art. It is recognised by the historian as one of the critical turning-points of the national record. It closed the door on projects which promised well, and diverted the course of ecclesiastical development from what seemed to be its natural channel. It opened a chapter of strife and confusion which has not even yet, after two and a half centuries, reached its close.   If on this occasion I take leave to direct your attention to that memorable and decisive moment in the history of our Church and Nation, my excuse must be that the circumstances of the present time almost compel a reconsideration of the policy which found enduring expression in the Act of Uniformity, and that it is the case that large numbers of our fellow-citizens are, for very intelligible reasons, recalling the events of 1662 with mingled feelings of pride and resentment, pride in the unyielding rectitude which marked the victims of the Caroline policy, resentment against the policy and its apologists. Anglicans and Nonconformists are at one in regarding the Act of Uniformity as the starting-point of their modern history ; and both are at the present time, for very different reasons, seeking to abrogate it. The Anglicans of the Caroline epoch did not scruple to speak of the Act of Uniformity as 'establishing' the Church of England; and those among us, who are least willing to concede much to the fact of Establishment, must needs allow that the Act of Uniformity created the very conditions, under which their dislike of Establishment finds respectable expression. The whole movement for 'Prayer Book Revision' is a movement for the abrogation of the clauses of the Act which stereotype the existing Book of Common Prayer. The whole agitation for Disestablishment is an agitation for the final abandonment of the policy which the Act enshrined. Thus both for Anglicans and for Nonconformists the Act of Uniformity is no half-forgotten and wholly obsolete statute, but an object of frequent and anxious consideration, which is forced on their notice by the circumstances of modern life. We may well inquire whether the events of that critical time do not disclose to the considering student some lessons which may help to guide him in the difficult situation which now confronts the English Churchman.

2. But, first, let me recognise and seek to remove an initial objection. What, it may be asked, is the use of moralising on the blunders of the past? To be wise after the event is no great advantage, and reflects no great credit. History is a process, of which the character and direction can only be discerned in retrospect. Nay, is it not a process, part of the general process, of natural evolution, with respect to which censure and approbation are alike improper, and the student's business is strictly limited to sifting evidence, and stating conclusions? 'Things will be what they will be,' though men fuss and fume to their hearts' content; and only our incorrigible vanity holds us back from perceiving that we have no more influence on the course of affairs than the proverbial fly on the cart-wheel. Why, therefore, should we sit in judgment on our ancestors, or cheat ourselves with

the notion that we have any immunity from the conditions of human action? We can but answer that such a mechanical view of history not only robs the study of ethical value, but also empties it of its highest interest. Moreover, it does not ring true to our own experience of life. ' History is past politics ; politics is present history,' was a saying of an Oxford historian of the last century, which was both characteristic and illuminating. It is not, indeed, the whole truth, but it is a very important part of the truth. We ought in reason to make our interpretation of human action in the past accord in point of method with our interpretation of human action in the present. We know well enough that the course of events, in which we ourselves are actors, is affected most powerfully by that original and incalculable force, which we conveniently speak of as personality. Behind the policies of the hour, which we can analyse, appraise, approve, and condemn, lies a hidden world of personal motive, which we can only guess at, never certainly know. When, indeed, we have succeeded in disentangling the personal factor, we only then find ourselves in presence of the real problem. Why that motive in that mind? Why so strange, and, as it seems to us, so perverse an estimate of values? Why so tragic a self-dedication to a single object, and that neither the most obvious, nor the most important, nor the most exalted? The bitter question of the Hebrew Sage might be written over the whole complicated drama of human life, of which the pages of history preserve the record, '*Who knoweth the spirit of man whether it goeth upward, and the spirit of the beast whether it goeth downward to the earth?*'

3. Yet the inexplicable is not necessarily also the unedifying. For, though there must be recognised in personality a factor which can never be brought within the categories of an intelligible evolution—for

'*The wind bloweth where it listeth, and thou hearest the voice thereof, but knowest not whence it cometh, and whither it goeth: so is every one that is born of the Spirit*'— yet men, as we know them, are for the most part—let cynics and pessimists say what they will—teachable and well-intentioned, erring more often from ignorance than from deliberate choice. History is the grand register of human achievements, and the ' Black Book' of human blunders, and therefore it is a storehouse both of precedents and of warnings. It is the shrine of a Deity whose oracles may be not rarely hard to understand, but which are never flattering or false. And if it be the case, as indeed it is, that ' History never really repeats itself,' and that, therefore, men can never rightly seek in the past precise directions for their present guidance, yet it is not less the case, that the most unchanging factor in human experience is man himself, and that the most trustworthy principles which he can follow are those which his own troubled course through the centuries has disclosed and illustrated.

4. The Restoration of the Monarchy in 1660 was justly regarded by our ancestors as an event so astonishing as almost to merit description as miraculous. For, after years of strife and confusion, men's hearts had been wonderfully softened, and the course of events strangely ordered, so that almost suddenly an event for which many had silently longed, but which had seemed to have fallen out of the realm of possibilities, actually happened. The King was brought back by the impulse of a common agreement, without formal conditions, but on an honourable understanding. What was that honourable understanding? Surely nothing less than that the new settlement of religion should be carried out in the same spirit of harmony and good-will as had prevailed in the Restoration itself. That honourable understanding received formal

expression in two Royal Declarations, and it was not openly repudiated until all political uses had passed out of it. Then free course was given to the vindictive passions, which exile and suffering had stirred in the minds of the triumphant Royalists, and a Settlement was effected, which was not only at the time grossly oppressive, but has left a legacy of division and resentment under which English life still suffers. An eminent Cambridge Historian, Professor GWATKIN, writing in a work which reflects honour on the historical students of this University, has pointed out that the persecution which followed this unhappy policy, lacked even the excuses which might have been urged for earlier persecutions. I take leave to quote his words :—

    ' Once again, and for the last time, England returned to the old ideal of a single national Church with no dissent allowed. And from that Church the Puritanism which had been struggling within it for the last century was now shut out by law. The national Church had been substantially national till it was narrowed into a party by LAUD : and now it was condemned to remain a party in the nation—no doubt the strongest party, but still not more than a party : for one whole side of the religious life of the nation was driven into opposition. So persecution assumed a new character. ELIZABETH might plead that the contest with Rome was in the main a struggle with foreign enemies for the very existence of Church and State in their national form ; and even LAUD might fairly say that the Puritans would put him down if he did not put them down. But there was no excuse of self-defence in 1662. The mass of the Nonconformists were no enemies of the Church, and desired no great changes in it: and, had they been ever so evil disposed, the Church was utterly beyond the reach of attack. BAXTER would have had no more chance against it than LUDO-WICK MUGGLETON. But, if there was no valid plea of self-defence, persecution was pure and simple revenge on the defeated party: and of mere revenge the better sort of churchmen would sooner or later be ashamed.' [1]

I think it would be true to say that in the interval of acute and difficult controversy which had elapsed since the downfall of the Established Church, many Anglicans had come to form definite convictions as to the necessity of episcopal government, and the invalidity of non-episcopal ministries, which assuredly were

[1] v. 'Cambridge Modern History,' vol. v. p. 330.

alien to the minds of the Reformers. In
their case I apprehend that the temptation
to which they yielded was not the comparatively coarse temptation of revenge,
but the more subtle temptation to ' *Do evil
that good might come.*' Circumstances had
brought to them an opportunity of en-
throning their principles in the National
Church by utilising the fierce passions
which swayed the victorious cavaliers.
To that temptation they yielded, and we
can now trace the miserable consequences
of their fault. ' *The wrath of man worketh
not the righteousness of God.*' Instead
of unifying the Church, they divided the
nation. No departure from their principles was required, for the Puritans were
prepared to accept episcopacy : only
justice to opponents, and faith in the
ultimate wisdom of doing justly. Their
failure ruined the religious unity to which
they attached so much importance, and so
discredited the ecclesiastical principles
which they professed that, after a brief

episode of domination, marked by the violences of the meanest persecution which history records, those principles fell into disregard even within the Established Church, and are still alien to the general belief of English Churchmen.

5. If we regard this miserable 'Settlement' from the point of view of its victims, the same lesson emerges. The Act of Uniformity marked the final failure of Puritanism. That masterpiece of perfidious violence could only have been carried on to the statute-book by a flood-tide of persecuting sentiment. What was it that created such a flood-tide? What else than the violence which the Puritans themselves had not scrupled to employ in the day of their own power, and in the interest of what they conceived to be the truth? Over the Interregnum, not less than over the Restoration, we may write the legend: '*The wrath of man worketh not the righteousness of God.*' Anglicans and Nonconformists must commemorate

the ejection of the 2,000 incumbents, who preferred indigence to infamy, with equal self-reproach, and confess their share in the great crime in terms of a common confession.

6. Perhaps, however, it would not be untrue to say that the error of the Puritans has more to teach us now than that of their opponents. For in truth it was a more generous error, and it belongs to a type of error which is never obsolete, whereas the gross error of the Anglicans is little likely to be defended or repeated in any recognisable form. Religious persecutors bid fare to become an extinct species, but social reformers are always with us; and while the Anglican of the Restoration was a religious persecutor inspired by political panic, the Puritan of the Commonwealth was a persecuting social reformer inspired by religious fervour. It will be worth our while to appreciate his error, and endeavour to trace its modern forms.

7. It is a commonplace to say that the fundamental weakness of Puritanism as a political creed lay in the fact that it assumed in a nation the ethical standards and ideals of a Church, and applied the coercive methods proper to the first in the interest of the last. Thus it was committed to a twofold blunder. It failed to build its social legislation on the only secure foundation, namely, the general will : and it failed to respect the essential condition of moral health, namely, individual liberty. By a process which was really inevitable, Puritanism in politics sank quickly into a hypocritical tyranny, equally feeble and irritating. Never were ideals loftier, or the self-dedication of men to them more complete and sincere, or the courage with which they were striven for more amazing, yet never was defeat more absolute and humiliating. The enthusiastic Puritan, aflame with his dream of a Kingdom of GOD on earth, could not by the purity and fervour of his zeal extricate

himself from the conditions under which
all men, saints and reformers as well as
the rest, must needs act in such a world
as this. Nor was it only in the political
sphere that his attempt to transcend the
limits of normal humanity was made, and
defeated. Within the narrower sphere of
his private life he made the same mistake,
and was overtaken by the same failure.
He could not permanently maintain himself at the level to which his occasional
ecstasies uplifted him. The prosaic
claims of ordinary existence laid hands
on him also, and, though his fervent
modes of speech and fantastic disciplines
of habit, might disguise from himself the
humbling fact, yet it was plain enough to
his neighbours that, save for some personal affectations, which were not attrac-
tive or intelligible to common folk, he was
really swayed by the familiar motives, and
in bondage to the conventional desires.
He seemed, therefore, to his critics and
victims less the exponent of an unearthly

virtue, than a dour shrewd man who 'made the best of both worlds.' When the crash came at the Restoration, and the whole edifice of Puritan legislation lay in ruins, none cared to remember the lofty ideal which had inspired it, in the joy of release from its actual burden.

8. Pass from the seventeenth century to the twentieth, from an age obsessed with theology to an age obsessed with economics, and observe how the Puritan Ideal emerges again, with the old excuses, and not less with the old incapacitating defects. The Kingdom of GOD shall be established on earth by the efforts of Christian men, and human society as a whole shall be dragooned into an acceptance of Christian principles—that, in brief, is the argument alike of the Christian Socialist and of the Puritan, and what does it really amount to more than the claim that ' *The wrath of man,*' that is, his overbearing zeal and passion of conviction,

'*shall work the righteousness of God*' in the sphere of economic life ?

9. No man can know anything of English society at the present time without recognising, as its salient and most honourable feature, a genuine horror at the hardships and inequalities of society, and an unselfish passion for social reform. Within the Christian Churches these sentiments are naturally clothed in religious phrases, and induce in many devout men an enthusiastic advocacy of economic change. In the Church of England a close observer might perhaps discern a revival of asceticism connecting itself with the new zeal for social equality : in the non-established Churches the reforming movement is more frankly political, but in both alike it implies a vehement revolt against the conditions under which industrial society, as we know it, exists, and a categorical demand that the economic process itself shall be frankly moralised. The rapid spread of

'Socialism' among the professedly religious sections of the people—a phenomenon which has a perplexing, and even a paradoxical aspect to those who perceive the essential divergence in principle and objective between 'Socialism' and historic Christianity—is to be explained by the direct challenge to existing conditions which 'Socialism' makes, and its insistent appeal from the harshness of economic 'law' to the fundamental demands of morality.

10. Arguing simply from the obvious fact that the desires of the individual reflect his volitions, the 'Christian Socialist' boldly postulates that the whole process of economic life is within human control, and draws the inference that the individual Christian must accept direct responsibility for the social anomalies which flow from industrial conditions. Earnest appeals are made to Christian men, as such, to repudiate for themselves a share in the current system, and by

organised effort to secure the triumph of righteousness in the economic sphere. 'White lists' of shopkeepers and employers, who reach the standard agreed upon as 'Christian,' are drawn up, and circulated ; public opinion is 'organised' against recalcitrants, and the attempt is openly made to moralise industry by main force. But this is not all. There is at hand a more potent instrument than the action of individuals and Churches. The State wields a power which no Church, nor all the Churches combined, can wield. A democratic State is very accessible to pressure from public opinion, liable to be carried away by waves of sentiment, little disposed to criticise proposals that fall in with its wishes. Moreover the State can coerce reluctant citizens, and enforce whatever policies it may approve. In effect, this is what is happening. A view and a treatment of economic problems which commend themselves to Christians, and which assume Christian convictions

and habits of living, are being advocated
as suitable for adoption by the nation as
a whole, and the State is in danger of
being carried on a wave of altruistic
sentiment to the acceptance of policies,
which have no real supports in the
opinions and habits of the people and
involve a disregard of economic conditions
which must ultimately prohibit success.
The mere attempt thus to impose a Christian standard on the nation is fertile in
moral anomalies.   It is to me a cause of
deep and continuing wonder that Christian people generally appear to regard
with so little concern the oppression of
individuals, which is now an accepted
method among those politicians who claim
to represent the labouring class.   No im-
provement of material circumstances could
really outweigh the injury to self-respect
involved in the triumph of those methods.
Surely the Christian Church at the
present time ought gravely and anxiously
to weigh the words of the SAVIOUR, and

Puritanism in England.   20

to consider the perpetual significance of
His attitude, when He deliberately refused to be made a party to the secular
conflicts of men, and preferred to point
them to the hidden roots of their trouble.
'*One out of the multitude said unto Him,
Master, bid my brother divide the inheri-
tance with me. But He said unto him,
Man, who made Me a judge or a divider
over you? And He said unto them, Take
heed and keep yourselves from all covetous-
ness; for a man's life consisteth not in the
abundance of the things which he pos-
sesseth.*'

11. I have ventured to indicate what
appears to me a remarkably significant
parallel to that memorable error of the
Puritans, which was so cruelly punished
250 years ago. You will not have failed
to notice that I have carefully avoided
reference to the question, which, however,
lies too near my argument to be wholly
ignored, whether indeed human life in
society be really conditioned by economic

'laws' which no ethical considerations can effect. At the conclusion of a sermon I cannot enter on the formal discussion of that painfully interesting question, yet I will not refuse the brief confession of my belief. Suffice it to say, then, that to my mind it is evident that the ultimately determining factors of economic life do lie outside the range of individual human volition, and therefore in a true sense are, so far as individuals are concerned, beyond moral control: that the influence of moral action on the economic process is far more restricted than enthusiasm is ready to admit, or pride willing to acknowledge : that the power of religion in the life of society, as in that of individuals, must be '*made manifest in weakness*' : that man, in the last result, must own the empire of economic, as of physical 'law' : that, notwithstanding, human character is really independent of circumstances : that, therefore, the future of mankind cannot really turn on the terrestrial fortunes of the race : that, to borrow sacred and familiar language, '*we have not here an abiding city, but we seek after the city which is to come :*' that '*our citizenship is in heaven.*' This is the faith which can sustain the human spirit under the cruel and baffling enigmas of life, and make evèn the stained and sombre records of history luminous with moral witness. Through the mighty madness of physical catastrophe, as through the heartless movements of economic evolution, and the bewildering maze of politics, I see a stage prepared on which the divine drama of personal life is being wondrously disclosed. '*The spirit of man is the candle of the Lord,*' and where that 'kindly light' is shining, under whatever conditions of gloom and danger, there I know myself to be in presence of the Shekinah Cloud itself. Elsewhere are darkness and the deep. '*Thy way is on the sea, and Thy paths on the great waters, and Thy footsteps are not known.*'

12. But my argument in this sermon is properly independent of these conclusions. Extend the range of human volition as widely as you will, bind together ethics and economics as closely as you can, and yet it will be the case that you can never escape from the divine law which St. JAMES has tersely affirmed in the text : ' *The wrath of man worketh not the righteousness of God.*' Violence can compel an attitude : it cannot inspire a faith. It can dictate a policy : it cannot alter facts. There is a true and indestructible connection between methods and results. ' *Do men gather grapes of thorns, or figs of thistles ?* ' We may not ' *do evil that good may come,*' because, if in the ardour of unreflecting zeal, or in the pride of individual ambition, or in the haste of an impatient enthusiasm, we surrender ourselves to that paradox, and cast into the furrows of society that malefic seed, we forfeit all prospect of any other harvest than that which belongs to

it. There is a 'natural law in the spiritual world' which may not be ignored with prudence, or violated with impunity. '*Be not deceived: God is not mocked, for whatsoever a man soweth, that shall he also reap. For he that soweth unto his own flesh shall of the flesh reap corruption; but he that soweth unto the Spirit shall of the Spirit reap eternal life.*'